D1013635

OTHER BOOKS BY JIM JORGENSEN

The Graying of America

Your Retirement Income

How to Stay Ahead in the Money Game

How to Make IRAs Work for You

MoneyShock

Money Lessons for a Lifetime

IT'S NEVER TOO LATE TO GET RICH

THE NINE SECRETS TO
BUILDING A NEST EGG
AT ANY AGE

FULLY REVISED AND UPDATED

Jim Jorgensen and
Rich Jorgensen

A Fireside Book
Published by Simon & Schuster
New York London Toronto Sydney Singapore

FIRESIDE
Rockefeller Center
1230 Avenue of the Americas
New York, NY 10020

This Fireside Edition 2003

Published by arrangement with Dearborn Financial Publishers

Fireside and colophon are registered trademarks
of Simon & Schuster, Inc.

For information regarding special discounts for bulk purchases,
please contact Simon & Schuster Special Sales
at 1-800-456-6798 or business@simonandschuster.com

Designed by Chris Welch

Manufactured in the United States of America

5 7 9 10 8 6 4

Library of Congress Cataloging-in-Publication Data
Jorgensen, James A.
It's never too late to get rich : the nine secrets to building a nest
egg at any age / Jim and Rich Jorgensen.
p. cm.
Originally published: Chicago : Dearborn Financial Pub., c1994.
Includes index.
1. Finance, Personal. 2. Saving and investment. 3. Retirement—United States—Planning. 4. Baby-boom generation—Finance, Personal. 5. Parents—Finance, Personal. 6. College costs.
I. Jorgensen, Rich (Richard). II. Title.
HG179 .J633 2003
332.024'01—dc21 2002191100

ISBN 0-7432-3749-8 (Pbk)

ACKNOWLEDGMENTS

We want to thank the many people who have made our trip through life meaningful and successful—people we have met at seminars and speaking engagements, and callers on the air who have helped make this book possible. We also want to thank Carol Renza, who has been my radio network affiliate director and without whom the radio show could not have stayed on the air; Dave Barry, who has been the producer of the radio show for the past seven years and who somehow keeps me focused and on the air; Debby Levine, our assistant, who runs the companies; and Easan Katir, who manages Portfolio Investing and is often co-host on the radio program.

We are also grateful to Tom Henry of Salomon Smith Barney in San Francisco; and to Lisa Considine, our coach and editor at Simon & Schuster in New York; and to our wives, Nancy and Sheri, who helped us remember what we learned in our life's work.

CONTENTS

INTRODUCTION

Know the value of a dollar, ponder it,
and hold on to that dollar tightly.
—Mark Twain

For most people, making a change in the way they do things is very scary. It transforms what is known into what is unknown. Yet in my talks around the country and on my nationwide radio show I often hear from people who tell me how the changes in this book have affected their lives.

Believe it or not, thousands of people have credited this little story about how I have invested and managed my money over my lifetime with turning their worry-free retirement dreams into reality.

The changes in the way you manage money may not be easy to put into practice, but like so many people who have read this book, once undertaken they can change your life and how you think about accumulating wealth. That's why I gave prepublication copies to my employees and to those who called in on my nationwide radio show. I wanted to share my story with them so they would know that change can bring success in their lives. Hundreds of people who have read the book have told me how helpful it was, how they have already made some changes, and that for the first time, they now see themselves managing their own money.

Sometimes fear of the future can be good. When you are afraid things could get worse, afraid you could lose even more money, it can prompt you to accept change. But at other times powerful emotions take over and cloud our judgment in deciding how to put our money to work. We are paralyzed by our own fears and we choose to remain in the past.

If we can change what we believe, we can change what we do. But if we can't learn new ways, we can fall behind and suddenly find that much of what we do makes us unhappy and unable to nourish our lives, and leaves us without the choices we seek for ourselves and our loved ones.

Money is often the soul of our well-being. We pursue it each workday because we believe it will make us happy. But if we get it and then lose it we're traumatized. Even if we get it and keep it, we may wind up with empty lives unless we reach out and touch someone.

With the explosion of online trading during the fabulous bull market of the 90s, everyone seemed to be making a killing in the stock market. The reality is that in most years more stocks lose money than make money. With today's soaring and plunging stock market, a lot of investors who jumped on the runaway technology boom in 2000 lost double-digit percentages in 2001.

Today, as I read my mail, look at my e-mail, and listen to the callers on my network radio show, I sense on a very personal level that for many people the scenario of riches shown on the TV dramas about Wall Street does not match their financial lives. They spend money so fast the inside of their wallet has skid marks. When they get a raise, they don't use the extra money to pay down their debt; they accumulate more! My answer to these concerns—and my motivation behind writing this book—is the firm conviction that, amidst the worry and anxiety over money, there is much that anyone can do to build and protect his or her financial security.

I've tried to cut out the small stuff that's not important and concentrate on what you really need to learn in your busy life, including what's worked for me over the years and my general philosophy of investing.

What are the most important things I've learned in life—things I've done each day that have put me on Easy Street as I head toward retirement? I've followed the basic rules I learned from growing up with the farmers in my small town, from my days on Wall Street, from my years on radio talking to people across America. As Mark Twain advised, I've learned the value of a dollar. You can learn these same things and use the knowledge to avoid most of your money problems later in life.

You may not agree with all the conclusions that I've drawn from my life's experiences, and obviously some are more important than others, but as my son told me, "Dad, the simple steps I take each day have let me forget about money problems. Now I'm adding my own experiences and someday I'll give them to my two sons."

I'm not going to claim to know everything—I only know what has worked for me (and what hasn't) over the past 40 years. A wise man once said, "If you want to know how you feel about something, remember your youth." So, let me tell you a little about mine.

I was born in Omaha, Nebraska (along with Warren Buffett), in what today would be called an *economically disadvantaged household.* I didn't know it at the time, but I did know, since my family did not own a car, that if I wanted to go someplace I had to make my own way. And when I went to a birthday party, I had to bring a gift. My mom usually bought the gift, but one day she gave me two dollars to buy one. "What can I buy?" I asked. She said, "Buy whatever you'd like, I'm sure Johnny will like it, too." I went to the store and found just what I'd always wanted. All I had to do then was convince my mom to let me keep it. I tried the ploy that Johnny might not like it and maybe we should get another gift. Mom didn't buy that. Then I said it had batteries and maybe we should open the package to make sure they were still good. Mom said we'd trust the batteries. I even tried to get sick the day of the birthday party in the hope that Mom would forget about the gift.

Do you know what it's like to give someone else a birthday gift that you've always wanted? That's the whole deal with birthday parties, except I never forgot that day and I vowed that someday I'd have enough money to buy the things I wanted.

Later in life, my family moved from Omaha to a small farming town of maybe 800 people. I learned my first basic money management lessons in high school when I visited my dad, who was an accountant at a farm machinery store. I can still remember pulling five-cent Cokes from a bucket of cold water and talking with the farmers. They all wore bib overalls and talked about the new tractors, the hay rakes, and about money. At first appearance these farmers didn't appear to be sophisticated money managers, but they always paid cash, drove big Cadillacs, and knew the value of a dollar saved.

I'll never forget the time I pulled up a chair and sat in front of an intimidating 250-pound, six foot tall farmer. He had power behind his voice when he said, "So you want to get rich?"

"Yes," I eagerly said.

"Well, remember this," he said. "Save some of your money to invest first, then spend what's left."

"Is that all?" I asked.

"Yes," he said. Then he got up, walked to the curb, and got in his Cadillac and drove away. I never saw him again.

It's possible this farmer learned from Benjamin Franklin, who in 1758 said, "For age and want save while you may; no morning sun last a whole day." I know I learned from this farmer, and his advice became the cornerstone of my effort to build a retirement nest egg.

When I went to college I discovered that business professors never talked to the farmers, never drove Cadillacs, and saved only a few dollars a month instead of creating investments. Maybe that's why none of them taught courses on getting rich. I learned how to accomplish that from the farmers.

My next lessons in basic money management came on Wall Street. The people you see on television running around waving their arms and throwing bits of paper on the floor of the New York Stock Exchange work at the world's greatest money machine. For the most part, they are rich. On the other hand, the briefcase-carrying people on the sidewalk outside worry about paying their mortgages and credit card bills. The reason is the traders at the exchange *make money work for them,* while the briefcase crowd *work for money.* This is a powerful concept and if you can put it to work, you'll grow richer than those who work for a living.

I also learned to hang on to my investments from watching the good stocks the traders loved bounce up and down but never fall off the table. I call them my *favorites.* On our radio show a caller asked: "Why do you always say 'stay in the market and stay invested'?"

"Because it works," I said.

"But that means I can't take advantage of the hot tips I get at the office and at cocktail parties."

"That's right," I said.

"Well, what if some of my stocks or funds are crashing and I'm losing tons of money?"

"Then you've invested in the wrong place," I replied gently.

"The good stuff won't crash, will always come back, and over time will make money."

For myself, I know sitting on good blue-chip stocks can make you rich. But the one time my roots of growing up in Omaha and following Warren Buffett failed me, I paid a big price! Had I invested $1,000 in Buffett's Berkshire Hathaway stock ten years after I graduated from college instead of sitting on my hands, the grand would be worth about $60 million today! You do the math yourself. In 1965 Berkshire Hathaway was worth $12 a share. On May 1, 2002, a share of stock was trading for $76,000.

Like every other author of a book on personal finance, I'm going to tell you to save part of your income first and invest in the stock market. The reason why this is so important may surprise you.

"Look," a trader on Wall Street told me, "*You can't make money on money you don't have.* If you spend it you don't have it. If you don't have it, you can't acquire the assets that will eventually make money for you."

"Is personal finance that simple?" I asked.

"Yes," he said, waving his hands at another trader on the floor. "People use their money to pay off debts like car loans and credit card bills. If they want to become rich they need to concentrate on acquiring assets like stocks and funds. For most people this is the only rule they need to remember," he said. "All they'll do is juggle bills until they reduce their debt and start acquiring assets."

Most people, including myself, have found it difficult to save before we spend. What helped me start saving was another conversation I had with a farmer.

"Look, sonny, if you don't pay yourself first, no one else will."

"Is that how you got rich?" I asked eagerly.

"That's it," he said, pulling on his bib overalls. "Lord knows you don't have to be smart, but if you don't save some money, all the fancy investment advice in the world won't make you rich."

"How did you learn to pay yourself first?" I asked.

"The problem most people face is that they can't pay themselves first because no one has sent them a bill. To get started, I made up a bunch of bills, put them in envelopes addressed to me and gave them to a friend. Each month, I got a bill in the mail and sent the money to the bank. After a while, I just included those bills with my mortgage and other payments, and I never missed the money."

Most of us already have experience with paying ourselves first. It's called *forced savings.* When we buy a life insurance policy or a new home, we are forced to save to meet the required payments. If you want to reduce your overall spending so that you can pay yourself first and have enough left to pay your monthly bills and expenses, follow the lead of the wealthy. They don't need to make a statement; they buy only what they need and travel with battered luggage.

Here are some ways to save a few dollars that could make a big difference in the size of your retirement nest egg:

Suggestion	**Estimated savings**	
Takeout instead of dining out once a month	$45 monthly	$540 yearly
One less trip to the car wash	$12 monthly	$144 yearly
Video rental instead of a movie	$11 monthly	$132 yearly
Take your lunch to work once a week	$24 monthly	$288 yearly
Put a dollar a day in the piggy bank	$30 monthly	$365 yearly

Just cutting out those few items could result in a savings of $1,469 a year. Let's say each month you put this money in a good mutual fund that over time earned a 15 percent average annual total return. In fifteen years, you could have $80,000 in your IRA or 401(k). Try that for twenty years and you could end up with about $175,000. And if you start when you are 35, *and this is your only retirement plan,* and you put $1,469 a year into a good stock fund to age 65, you might end up with about $730,000 when you reach age 65!

But there is something deeper at work here. If you start at age 35 and make the $1,469 contribution to your IRA each year, you will have socked away about $44,000 to age 65. Over the years, however, you have a gain of about $686,000. In this example, only about 6 percent of the money came from your annual contributions, and 94 percent came from compounding over time! That's the way to build a retirement nest egg! Over those thirty years you are saving toward retirement *your average annual gain was about $22,860 on a $1,469 annual contribution!*

But the most important step in making this money machine work for you is to take action. *Don't be afraid to start now.* As you spend your money, be positive and think success. If you can do these things, you can turn your dreams into reality. Then your power of determination will do the job. Be like the 73-year-old man who made a 240-mile trip to visit his 80-year-old brother, who was ill, driving his lawn mower all the way. He chose to use his John Deere riding mower as his vehicle because he didn't have a driver's license. Hitched to the back of the mower was a trailer in which he hauled supplies and camping equipment. He averaged only five miles an hour, and the trip took six weeks.

What I discovered a long time ago, along with the man on the lawn mower, is that if you really want to do something, chances are you can. Financial success is a lifelong marathon, not a sprint that lasts a few years. Whatever your goals may be—saving for college, a new car, a new home, or retirement—set up separate accounts and add to them each month. That way, you'll know exactly what you're aiming for and why you are paying yourself first while the spendthrifts run wild at the local department store. Let me say again one of the most important things I learned on Wall Street:

It's *not* how much money you make each month that counts, it's how much you save and invest each month that counts.

They don't teach this in school, but if you don't learn it, you can become a slave to bill paying and empty pockets.

EACH OF US has a choice to make every day regarding our attitude. We cannot change our past. We cannot change the inevitable. The only thing we can do is rely on what we have—our attitude. I'm convinced that life is 10 percent what happens to us and 90 percent how we react to it. After all, your trip to financial success should be as much fun as arriving at the destination.

Today, however, we receive overwhelming amounts of frequently contradictory information, which (we are told) we must understand if we are to keep up with the times. But most of us read this mass of information without comprehending, see it without learning how to use it, and hear it without understanding its ramifications. In reality, there are ever-widening gaps between what we understand, what we think we understand, and what we're told we should understand. We are often stuck with the come-ons that play to our ego and promise to simplify investing.

As a result, many people who ask me for advice on where to invest their extra money are not ready to make investments. They have become financially bogged down because they continue to make the most common mistakes in personal finance: paying too much interest, failing to set up a tax-deductible retirement plan, failing to buy enough life and disability insurance, and passing up opportunities to save money. Often they've heeded the advice of investment gurus who offer the latest surefire undiscovered stock, a way to double your earnings in some remote corner of the earth, or the impossible dream of high returns with low risk.

The good news for most of us is that the stock market has risen more in our lifetimes than ever before. The Dow Industrial Average was only 777 in 1982. In just eighteen years, at the start of this century, it had soared to over 11,000. And that's just the beginning. The computer revolution will spawn a never-ending array of high-tech products to provide us with tiny sensors embedded in almost everything we use. We'll have music from the Net, cars that get a hundred miles per gallon, cell phones that become personal computers and connect to the Internet, and home appliances that are controlled by our voices.

So get set for the next decade. You will need to stay invested in stocks and look upon any short-term market setbacks or changes in your career as opportunities to grow into a new environment of change. You will need to continually redesign how you live and work, but you will live through the greatest economic boom in our nation's history.

The Power Is in Your Hands

I sincerely believe that if you follow these nine steps to financial freedom, you can quit worrying about your future retirement nest egg. Instead, when you retire, you'll have the money to play golf, take the grandkids to Disneyland, and enjoy life. There are no guarantees, of course, but after years of working with people and helping them plan their financial futures I am convinced that what

I have done (and what I suggest you do) is the best overall plan to build your financial security.

Over the years I've learned that the most important things you can do in life are to make yourself happy, to share your love and understanding with your family, and to take each day one day at a time.

I hope each time you re-read this book you'll find something new and useful for yourself, your loved ones, and your friends. I'm glad that I can share what I've learned and I wish you well as you build your financial future.

STEP 1

Follow the Basic Rules

Eighty to 90 percent of the money in your ultimate retirement nest egg will be money you never saved or invested.

Most people tell me they are shocked when I say this on radio or television, but it's true! When I understood this I realized that no matter how small of an investment I could make, the money could grow to be a big part of my retirement nest egg. I don't care if you raid a cookie jar or hide the money under your mattress. If you can save pennies a day and invest them on a regular basis, you can start your journey toward millionaire status.

Hidden Money on Your Way to Work

Let's say you can save 500 pennies a day—about the cost of a cup of coffee and a roll at Starbucks. Now, if you can save the 500 pennies five days a week for a year, you'll have saved $1,300. If you invest that entire wad of cash, leave it alone, and never make another investment, and you earn 13 percent a year for the next fifteen years (from 1980 to the end of 1999 the average annual return for large cap stocks was 17.87 percent), your pennies could grow to more than $8,000. Keep the pennies invested another five years, or twenty years overall, and your pile of cash could have grown to more than $15,000.

The secret of compounding: You not only earn money on your new investment, but you also earn money on your entire previous balance.

Now let's assume you save and invest 500 pennies each workday *each year* over the next fifteen years. Again, assuming the same investment returns, this "Let's get started with 500 pennies a day investment program" could be worth about a cool $60,000! Do this for twenty years and you're on your way to becoming rich. Your investment account could total a whopping $120,000.

Let me say again, one of the most important points you need to understand in building wealth is that most of the money you accumulate in your lifetime will be money you never saved or invested in the first place. Take our simple investment program, saving and investing 500 pennies each workday and investing $1,300 each year over twenty years. The total piggy bank money you saved over this twenty-year period was $26,000. Yet under this example, your retirement nest egg could total $120,000—nearly five times the money you actually saved! No one's going to throw away 500 pennies a day, but you might sit up and take notice if over twenty years these pennies could turn into a gain of $94,000 ($120,000 less $26,000 invested). If you divide that figure by twenty years, you have had an average annual buildup of $4,700 on a piggy bank savings plan of just $1,300 a year! That's almost four times your annual contribution each year!

Most of America's greatest fortunes have been made through the magic of compounding. It's true those early millionaires avoided income taxes and often made business deals without regard for the public good, but once they had the money, compounding it over time is what made them wealthy. Today, the same principle is at work in your individual retirement accounts and your company retirement plans. In fact, the secret to making money could be summed up in just these five words:

Learn the importance of compounding.

Let's say you start by putting a penny on your dresser. Each night thereafter you double the number of pennies on the dresser. After ten days, you'd have $5.12. By continuing to double the number of pennies each night, you'd reach $163.84 by the fifteenth night. But in just five more days, you'd need a big dresser top. The pile of pennies would now total $10,485.76. At the twenty-fifth day, the amount will have grown to $167,772.16. At the end of thirty days, the pile of pennies has taken over your bedroom. You now have a total of $5,368,709.12. In just a few more weeks, you'd have every penny in the country on your dresser top.

You may be tiring of my telling you how important compounding is to building wealth, but consider it on indication of how critical this concept is to your getting rich. This time let's look at how hard your money works for you. Say you invest $1,000 and never add to your initial investment.

	Total Return			
End of Year	5%	8%	10%	15%
5	$1,276	$1,469	$1,610	$2,011
10	1,628	2,159	2,594	4,046
15	2,079	3,172	4,177	8,137
20	2,653	4,661	6,727	16,367
25	3,385	6,848	10,835	32,919
30	4,322	10,063	17,449	66,218

This table illustrates that the most important factor in building wealth is the total returns you earn each year.

Let's say you invested $10,000 on June 30, 1991, in a stock mutual fund earning 15 percent a year; by June 30,2001, your account would have grown to about $40,000. However, had you played it safe in an 8 percent bond fund, you'd have about $20,000, or half the money earned in the stock fund. Even safer, investing in a federally insured 5 percent certificate of deposit, your money could have grown only $16,000. The point is, you can choose where to invest your money, and over the years I've found that:

You'll never get rich with a single-digit savings account.

Let's assume you squirrel away $2.74 a day in a cookie jar and invest $1,000 each year. Depending on where you put your money, you could end up with anywhere from almost $70,000 to almost half a million dollars!

End of Year	Total Invested	Total Return			
		5%	8%	10%	15%
5	$5,000	$5,802	$6,336	$6,716	$7,754
10	10,000	13,207	15,645	17,531	23,349
15	15,000	22,657	29,324	34,950	54,717
20	20,000	34,719	49,423	63,002	117,810
25	25,000	50,113	78,854	108,182	244,712
30	30,000	69,761	122,346	180,943	499,957

I call this *tortoise investing.* Like a tortoise, compounding takes time to cross the road, but with its steady progress, it will reach its goal. *Jackrabbit investing,* on the other hand, often zips here and there and never reaches the other side of the road. The sooner you start socking away money each month, the greater the effect compounding has on your future wealth. For a sure fire saving strategy, start small, start now, stick to it, and let the magic of compounding help do the job.

For as Long as You Can

The secret is to compound your money for as long as you can. Here's why: Let's say you can pay yourself first and save $200 a month. With an annual total return of 15 percent a year, in twenty years your account could total about $283,000. If you invest that same $200 a month for only fifteen years, you'll have only about $131,000 in the account.

Here's what the magic of compounding over time tells us:

- **Lesson 1.** The additional five years, with only another $12,000 saved and invested between the fifteenth and twentieth year, resulted in the return of an extra $140,000 ($152,000 less $12,000).
- **Lesson 2.** Since you effectively earn money on your money, you get a whopping *$28,000 average annual buildup* in your nest egg for continuing to save and invest only $2,400 each year for five more years. Let's face it, there's nothing thrilling about watching the slow but steady growth of your money through compounding. On the other hand, if you give it enough time it can make you a mountain of cash you won't outlive.

Since compounding works well over time, consider the benefits for your kids and grandkids. Say you have a child or grandchild who is at least 18 years of age. You'd like to make him or her a millionaire by the age of 65. What can you do? You can open an IRA for the young person and put the awesome power of compounding to work.

So long as the child or grandchild in question has $2,000 of earned income a year (contributions to an IRA can be 100 percent of earned income, up to a maximum of $3,000), you can then make a gift of $2,000 to their IRA. If you do this for eight years, or a total of $16,000, assuming an annual return of only 10 percent, when the child reaches age 65, compounding could have built the value of the IRA to over a million dollars.

Now let's find out how much you need to invest to have a cool million at age 65. The following chart shows the one-time and monthly investments needed to accumulate $1,000,000 by age 65, based on a 12 percent average annual return:

Age	One-time Investment	Monthly	Investment Value at 65
20	$6,098	$59	$1,000,000
25	10,748	104	1,000,000
35	33,378	328	1,000,000
40	58,823	594	1,000,000
50	182,696	2,121	1,000,000

If the monthly figures seem daunting, don't despair. Contribute what you can. If you are 40 years old, you could accumulate $250,000 by age 65 by investing $14,706, or $149 a month.

Does compounding work only when you invest money? No. You can also build equity in your home by saving on interest—the reverse of earning money through compounding. Most lenders make it easy to send in extra money each month on your mortgage payments by checking the box for extra principal payments. You can do this on a regular basis or whenever you have the extra cash.

Before you dismiss this idea, consider this: Just paying an additional 25 cents a day on an average thirty-year fixed mortgage at 8 percent can save you more than $7,000 in interest costs over the life of the loan. Marc Eisenson, author of *The Banker's Secret,* says, "Just imagine what you can do saving 50 cents a day and paying that on your mortgage. The average savings, over the term of the mortgage, is about $15,000. If you can save $1 a day, you'll save about $26,000." (For more information write The Banker's Secret, Box 78, Elizaville, NY, 12523, or call 914-758-1400.)

You will also reduce your mortgage term by sending in these extra monthly payments. Here are the extra amounts you'd need to pay each month to pay off a thirty-year fixed-rate mortgage at 7 percent early:

Loan Amount	To Pay off the Loan in 25 Years	To Pay off the Loan in 20 Years	To Pay off the Loan in 15 Years
$75,000	$31.11 extra	$82.50 extra	$175.15 extra
100,000	41.47 extra	109.99 extra	233.52 extra
160,000	66.36 extra	175.99 extra	373.64 extra
200,000	82.95 extra	219.99 extra	467.05 extra

SOURCE: Marc Eisenson, *The Banker's Secret.* New York, Villard Books, 1990.

Even if you don't plan to live in the home for thirty years, paying off your mortgage early will give you more equity whenever you're ready to sell. It's like making a down payment on your next home before you buy.

The Race to the Good Life

Instead of saving a few pennies each day, however, millions of Americans have joined the race to live the good life and they are burying themselves under a mountain of credit card bills. In fact, most young people aren't saving enough to meet the so-called triple squeeze: the cost of college, health care, and retirement. You know what I'm talking about: That pit in your stomach that tells you each day that you're living from paycheck to paycheck, that your personal finances resemble a bowl of spaghetti in mid-explosion, and that you have no idea how to break the cycle that leads to accumulating even greater debt.

For most people, going into debt brings on a case of denial. One reason, say retirement planners, is that most people have an exaggerated opinion of what their company pension and Social Security will be worth. They're kidding themselves into believing they have lots of time to save for retirement, college expenses, and family emergencies. In fact, in the decade of the double zeros, the pension gravy train has already left the station. Today the responsibility for retirement security has been transferred from the employers' paid pension plans to employee-funded 401(k) and IRA plans.

For today's sandwich generation, squeezed between caring for themselves, their children, and often their parents, this is a scary world. And the frightening thing is that the Generation Xers have not learned from the mistakes of the baby boomers. Credit card bills and overspending have prevented them from profiting during a long period of double-digit returns on Wall Street.

Today, only about 20 percent of the Americans born in the baby boom years between 1946 and 1964 are socking away enough money to retire anywhere near their current standard of living. The older baby boomers, those born between 1946 and 1956, will need to triple their savings rate just to maintain their standard of living after they turn 65. That, however, is an increasingly unlikely scenario given that about 70 percent of married people ages 51 to 61 have four-generation families—themselves, an elderly parent, and children who have children of their own. Another 25 percent have three-generation families. In years to come, today's couples probably will need to give financial assistance to their children *and* their parents.

Unfortunately, for many people the sum total of their financial planning consists of hoping that one day the phone will ring with the news that Uncle Henry died and left them 5 million. These folks spend, dream, wait for Uncle Henry's money, and then find at the end of the month that there's nothing left to save. Here are some shocking facts: Nearly half the employees eligible for their company's 401(k) plan don't contribute anything. More than 70 percent of all working Americans don't even have a modest emergency fund to tide them over if they lose their job or can't work.

People have the most imaginative rationalizations for spending now and delaying savings. One of the strangest is that they believe Social Security will support them in retirement. Currently the Social Security Administration says that 13 percent of all retirees have no other income but their monthly benefit checks. An additional 24 percent rely on Social Security for 90 percent or more of their total income in retirement.

If you think you can live on Social Security benefits when you turn 65, consider this:

You have no guaranteed rights to Social Security benefits.

You may not be aware that the huge amount of taxes zipping out of your paycheck each month for Social Security pays for a system that has never made any guarantees to you! As the replica of the original Social Security notice on page 22 makes clear from the very start: *"There is no guarantee that the funds thus collected will ever be returned to you."* Already underway are reductions in the replacement ratio and an increase in the age at which you collect benefits.

NOTICE

Deductions from Pay Start Jan. 1

Beginning January 1, 1937, your employer will be compelled by law to deduct a certain amount from your wages every payday. This is in compliance with the terms of the Social Security Act, sponsored and signed by President Roosevelt, August 14, 1935.

The deduction begins with 1%, and increases until it reaches 3%.

There is no guarantee that the fund thus collected will ever be returned to you. What happens to the money is up to each congress. No benefits of any kind before 1942.

This is NOT a voluntary plan. Your employer MUST make this deduction. Regulations are published by the Social Security Board, Washington, D. C.

Reducing the Replacement Ratio

The value of any pension plan is based on the amount of your preretirement salary that the plan replaces in retirement benefits. Though it's a wildly unpopular notion, lowering Social Security benefits is easy; the government need only reduce the replacement ratio. And in fact, the Social Security replacement ratio falls dramatically as income increases. For example, if you were an average earner your replacement ratio could be around 43 percent. If you had earned the maximum income on which Social Security taxes were withheld, the replacement ratio might be only 24 percent of your salary. If you were a high earner ($200,000), the replacement ratio could fall to only 8 percent. (Note that your actual monthly benefit is calculated from your entire work history and your payments into the system, and this is only an example of how your benefits might compare to your last working salary.)

Raising the Retirement Age

Congress has already set in motion plans to raise the age at which you can collect Social Security benefits. If you were born before 1938, your *normal retirement age* (the age at which you can collect full benefits) continues to be age 65, with benefits reduced to 80 percent for those who retire early at age 62. If you were born after 1938, your normal retirement age gradually increases. For example, a worker born in 1943 will receive full benefits at age 66, but one born in 1960 or later will have to wait until age 67.

Taxing the Benefits

Not long ago Congress repealed one of the worst aspects of the Social Security laws, the so-called earnings test for those over age 65. These retirees can now earn as much money as they want, pay ordinary income taxes *and Social Security taxes* on these earnings, and not lose any of their Social Security benefits. Those who retire between age 62 and 64 are still subject to an earnings test and a possible loss of benefits. Therefore, you shouldn't plan to collect Social Security before age 65 unless you'll have little or no earned income.

What about the other tax? Congress has slapped a tax on up to half of the Social Security benefits received by many taxpayers when their adjusted gross income exceeds $25,000, or $32,000 for married couples filing jointly. But for so-called high income taxpayers, 85 percent of benefits can be subject to taxes when adjustable gross income is over $34,000 single, or $44,000 for married couples filing jointly. The earnings under this test include all earned income, including income from tax-free bonds, dividends, and retirement plan payouts.

What will affect more retirees in the years to come is that the income levels that trigger taxes on Social Security benefits are not indexed for inflation. If retirees withdraw more money from their retirement plans or pensions to keep up with inflation, they could get hammered by the double taxes on their benefits.

Many workers who have paid taxes on earnings they contributed into Social Security each month during their working lives wonder why they have to pay income taxes once again on the benefits they receive. That's why so many have opened Roth IRAs, on which you pay taxes on the contributions you make into the plan, but not on withdrawals.

The Effects of Inflation

The mythological Greek character Sisyphus was condemned to Hades with the fate of repeatedly rolling a huge stone up a hill, only to have it roll down again each time. People who earn savings account interest for retirement or college expenses will also struggle mightily, like Sisyphus, to keep an enormous stone from rolling back over them and flattening the spending power of their money.

It might not matter to you that the price tag for a Rolls-Royce Cornice IV convertible jumped 6 percent in one year to about $285,000, or that the cost of imported chocolate truffles have increased about 10 percent a year, but it will matter to you what you pay for college costs, groceries, car insurance, and medical care in the years to come. I can remember the Great Depression, when inflation worked in reverse and prices fell. From that experience of being poor, I still pick up pennies from the street. I don't need the money, and today inflation has made the penny almost obsolete, but a lifetime of saving has instilled in me the belief that a *penny found is a penny saved.*

Remember your first monthly salary? Today, it might cover your monthly grocery bill. Callers to my radio show tell me that by the time their kids go to college, the cost of their education will be beyond their reach. Over the last decade, for example, the cost of a college education has risen twice as fast as the rate of family income, but our savings rate has not kept up with inflation.

It hasn't been much fun watching prices rise at your grocery store or gas station. The hard fact is that this rise in the price of goods and services can steadily eat away at your purchasing power and income. That's because:

Money is worth only what it will buy when you spend it.

Why Some Investors Never Beat Inflation

Suppose you had saved $20,000 in 1980 toward your future retirement nest egg. Over the next two decades, your 5 percent savings account could have grown to $53,000. Now let's suppose you are in a 28 percent tax bracket and your taxes totaled $14,800 over this period. Your net after tax investment could now total about $38,000. Over this twenty-year period, your initial $20,000 investment would have had to grow to about $36,000 just to keep pace with rising inflation. Your money is barely keeping up! By these standards, the savvy investor is the one who took a risk on the stock market and not someone who locked up *absolute safety* in a savings account.

Once you retire and the paycheck stops, however, you'll face another challenge: supporting yourself for many more years than you may have planned for. A 62-year-old retiree today is expected to live another twenty-two years. The earlier you plan to retire, the longer your money may have to last. Since you'll have less time to let compounding work to meet your goal, figure on boosting your annual savings and investments by about 5 percent for each year before age 65 that you plan to retire.

Now that you know how to overcome that paralyzing fear in the pit of your stomach brought on by the idea that you can't build up a sizable nest egg to overcome future inflation, the rest is easy. In fact, the good news is that you don't have to become a phenomenal stock picker or find a few lucky investments. All you have to do is follow the time-honored rule of saving money first, allowing compounding to work for you, and investing in good long-term stocks and mutual funds.

I said at the beginning of this chapter that using the magic of compounding to gain wealth was simple, but boring. At the risk of driving you crazy with a repeat of the same basic game plan, suppose that you had invested $10,000 in a mutual fund that had an annual overall total return of about 12 percent a year. Fifteen years later, the awesome power of compounding could have turned the original $10,000 investment into about $55,000.

What should be flashing through your mind is this: The gain of $45,000 works out, on average over the fifteen-year period, to be an annual buildup of about $3,000 on your original $10,000 investment. That, my friend, is a hefty *30 percent average annual gain each year.* And all you did was sit on your hands. This potential gain should snap into sharp focus the next time you think about investing some money.

Now I want you to follow my formula for sound money management.

Establish a budget

For many people, the word *budget* means skimping, passing up the good times, and depriving themselves of the fun in life. But with a sound budget you can get more—not less—out of the money you earn. A budget that lets you save first should also provide a cash reserve when an emergency strikes. Therefore, your first step should be to establish an emergency fund equal to at least four months' income. For this safety net, don't keep four months' living expenses in a checking account. Instead, keep the money in a money-market mutual fund or a higher-yielding short-term bond mutual fund. After that, the money you save might go into separate funds to pay off your personal debts or make the down payment on a car, or you might put the entire sum into a down payment on a home.

Without a workable budget, free-spenders will bag groceries after they retire.

You should also consider opening a home-equity credit line in advance of need, while you have a good job, and then keep it for emergency use. After a financial setback, the bankers will probably slam the door in your face. A second option is to draw on your individual investments in mutual funds. If you have a profit in securities, you'll be hit with taxes, but if you've lost your job, your income could be less, and it might be a good time to realize the gain. As a last resort, make withdrawals from your tax-qualified retirement plans.

Here are some points to consider as you put together a budget:

- **Put your budget in writing.** Keep it in a visible place where you can continually check up on your progress. A budget put away in a drawer is a dead budget.

- **Amend your budget as necessary.** No matter how dedicated you are to staying within your budget, your life and personal finances will change and you'll have to make adjustments.
- **Stay within your budget each month.** Devise a budget that is workable for your current situation and then develop the discipline to stick with it. My recommendation is to save 10 percent of your monthly income for retirement plan contributions and personal investing, but you can work up to that level as you develop your saving habits.

  Here's a guideline you can use for family finances: Most mortgage lenders have a maximum limit of 28 percent of gross income for mortgage payments, taxes, and insurance, and no more than 36 percent of monthly pretax income for all personal debt.

Pay off your personal debt

Does your credit card pop out of your wallet as if it were hooked up to radar when you approach a shopping center? I know people whose monthly statement looks as if they've been on a spending spree through Monte Carlo. Many of them find it impossible to pay off their credit card balance each month. These are clear signals that these people are on a treadmill to financial disaster. Once they bite the bullet and pay off their personal debt, they tell me they are surprised how easy it is to find the money to invest. In short, I *want you to become a savvy manager of credit with a zero balance each month!* Why?

Let's say you have $100 in credit card debt and $100 invested in an insured certificate of deposit paying 5 percent a year. The cost of $100 of credit card debt, at the national average card interest rate of 18 percent, is $18 a year, but you'll need to earn, in a 30 percent tax bracket, about $26 to pay the non-deductible credit card interest expense.

The income from $100 in an insured CD earning 5 percent will return $5.00 at the end of the year. The after-tax return is about $3.50. If you withdraw the $100 from the savings account and pay off the credit card debt, you would be ahead about $22.50 at the end of the year. Or to put it another way, if you are racing along the freeway of prosperity earning $3.50 while you're paying out $26, you are headed for a big-time financial crash!

Don't spend before you save—you can't retire on someone else's savings!

Pay yourself first

Once you've established a workable budget and eliminated your high-interest debt, you can begin to pay yourself first. Remember, your goal is 10 percent of your earnings. That doesn't mean you have to do that from day one. It will probably be easier for you to phase in your self-payments, beginning with 5 percent and then increasing the amounts until you reach your goal of 10 percent. Don't even think about the money that has already come off the top. If you are going to succeed in controlling your expenses and finding real wealth, you need to treat goal-setting as a serious and important business. Moreover, you must set your goal high enough to do the job and then have the desire to turn your dreams into reality.

If you are afraid to fail, you will succeed at failure.

Buy adequate insurance

Your next priority in building financial security is to protect yourself and your family with adequate life and long-term disability insurance. Even though life insurance protection is very inexpensive, most of the people I talk with at my investment seminars want to *invest* for the future before they *protect* their future.

Safeguard your money

Unlike our fathers, who were likely to stay with a company for thirty years and retire with a gold watch and a pension, this generation of workers will change jobs as many as eight or ten times, will change careers as many as three times in their lives, and will retire *without a traditional company pension,* according to the U.S. Department of Labor. If you don't roll over your company retirement plan assets into an IRA each time you change your job, you won't have a retirement nest egg at all.

Take advantage of your employer's retirement plan

If you don't take maximum advantage of these plans, it's like giving a big chunk of your money to the IRS. If you are self-employed, consider Keogh plans and SEP-IRAs. Regardless of which tax-deferred plan you select, start contributing now. It will require a small sacrifice each month in the form of payroll deductions, but with the magic of compounding and forced saving, you can end up with a sizable sum for your retirement years.

Be willing to accept some risk

One of the biggest problems most people face when they invest for their retirement is the fear of losing their hard-earned capital. As a result, billions of dollars are slumbering in low-yielding insured savings accounts, CDs, and Treasury bills. After paying taxes on their income from these "safe" savings, many investors actually lose purchasing power over the years.

There are two kinds of risk:

- **Risk or Volatility**

  A thousand dollars invested in a federally insured CD has no investment risk. It is certain to return the original $1,000 at maturity. There is also no volatility, since the investment is always worth $1,000.

- **Risk and Volatility**

  Investing in bonds and the stock market, on the other hand, carries the risk of the loss of principal, especially if you withdraw your money within a one- or two-year period. But there is also volatility, since the market value of the investment can change from day to day.

When you put your money in a savings account, you pay for the lack of risk and volatility by giving up any opportunity for appreciation of your investment.

The loss of appreciation is the major factor in sharply reducing the size of your ultimate retirement nest egg.

If you seek to preserve your capital by choosing investments with the lowest volatility, you'll find, as you read the papers each day, that the market value of your investment has changed very little. You are free from the market's sharp downturns and you relax in the belief that your capital is safe. For long-term investors, however:

Change is the key to building wealth.

With an investment in stocks, the market value may soar or plunge from day to day or week to week, but it's this volatility over the years that build nest eggs.

My advice to you: Don't obsess over the small stuff, when a wonderful lifestyle could be within your reach. Or, to put it another way, you can't make it to retirement on the beach with an average 5 percent yearly return, but you'll be able to dance the night away with an average annual return of 15 percent.

Your job—what may appear to many investors as a mission impossible—is to be courageous and realize that when an ugly bear market occurs, as it did in 1973–1974, in the big crash in 1987, in the mini-downturn during the Gulf War in 1991, and in the meltdown of the Dow Industrials and the Nasdaq market in 2000/2001, you should sit on the beach and simply watch the surf.

Keep your hands off your investments

Tom Henry, a broker with Salomon Smith Barney in San Francisco, told our radio listeners that "People are their own worst enemy. They look at a short-term market fluctuation like a major correction and they think that proves, shall we say, that the world can come to an end. That's like saying a rainy day just proves that agriculture can't work. You have to take a longer view.

"If you take the infinite viewpoint, which I recommend, just buying and never planning on selling, you should do very well. Hopefully I'm reaching the people who haven't yet made the move into the stock market. A market downturn will come for them, and from my experience, that's the time to keep your investments in place like you were wearing lead shoes."

After thirty years of watching investors rush from fund to fund, from hot stock to hot stock, from oil to gold to biotech, to the latest bond or stock fund invested in a country somewhere south of the equator, I have observed that most investors lose money while their financial advisers pay off big mortgages and buy BMWs.

The problem is that most people feel they have to be doing something or accepting someone's advice to make money with their investments. Again, let me ask you to keep another old Wall Street saying in mind when you're tempted to more your money from one investment to another at a moment of crisis:

The investment that requires the least intervention over time will produce the best results.

Today we live in a world in which millionaires are a dime a dozen. Never in our history have so many people made so much money so quickly. However, for most of us to become millionaires we have to earn the money the hard way. We also have to accept the fact that saving for retirement is up to each of us. We can't depend on Social Security, a company-pension, some rich uncle, or slots in a casino. Our retirement nest egg relies upon our ability to save and invest our own money over our lifetimes.

This isn't a new thought. Remember Aesop's fable about the ants and the grasshopper? As the story goes, the industrious ants worked night and day, storing food away for the coming winter. And all the while, the foolish grasshopper strummed away and called the ants a bunch of silly fools. When winter arrived, the shivering grasshopper came begging for some bread and the ant said, "Sorry, but you should have stored away some food. There's none to spare."

My own philosophy is that you don't have to live like the plodding ant in order to build your financial future, provide your children with an education, and assure your own comfortable retirement. You can dance and make music like the grasshopper so long as you manage your money wisely and let your money make money for you.

What I want you to do is change your lifestyle to incorporate these basic steps to financial security:

1. Establish a budget.
2. Pay off your personal charge-account debt.
3. Pay yourself first.
4. Buy adequate life and disability insurance.
5. Safeguard the money you've already saved.
6. Take full advantage of retirement plan opportunities.

7. Be willing to accept some risk.
8. Leave your investments alone and let time work for you.

The good news is that in spite of what you see on television or read in the papers, the basic rules for financial success have not changed. But they will work only if you take action, accomplish these basic steps and, most important of all, make up your mind that you want to become rich. I hope you find your dream of financial independence. I know you have the opportunity to do so.

STEP 2

Don't Be a Lender

Lenders take a big risk on what their money will buy in the future.

Individuals have lent money in return for interest payments since money was invented. It was not until 1472, however, when what many consider to be the oldest bank in the world, the Monte dei Paschi di Siena in Italy, introduced the forerunner to the passbook savings account. The idea that banks could attract individuals' savings and keep track of their accounts opened the door to massive lending. In Renaissance times, bankers like the Medicis and the Fuggers, with their state-licensed money machine to attract depositors' money, grew immensely wealthy.

Beyond the Passbook

The passbook savings account remained the principal mode of individual savings for almost five hundred years, until the advent of computers after World War II. The first stage of the ongoing technological revolution was internal. Since banks and thrifts are nothing more than giant counting houses, it was easy to run the entire customer list past the computer each day. Earned interest, which had been posted once a month or once a quarter, could now be posted every night. It was a small step, to be sure, but in the merchandising of money, it was a fundamental innovation.

In 1969, an enterprising young executive of the Worcester Five Cents Savings Bank petitioned the Massachusetts Banking Department for permission to offer a negotiable order of withdrawal account. A NOW account was, in effect, a computer-driven checking account that paid interest on the balance in the account. The executive knew he was skating on thin ice because at that time it was illegal for federally insured banks and savings and loans to pay interest on any monies on deposit for less than thirty days. However, the Massachusetts savings banks had their own deposit insurance fund, and Massachusetts law did not have the same tight restrictions as those that governed the federally insured banks and thrifts.

The state bank regulators gave his suggestion of using computers to track interest rates on checking accounts a frigid reception and turned him down cold, but the enterprising executive believed he had found a formula that could pry open the regulatory gate. He sued and he won. Thereafter, it became possible for state-chartered savings and loans to offer checking accounts that paid interest. For the first time since the advent of banking in the late 1400s, banks faced competition for the "free" money their customers had been forced to keep in non-interest-bearing checking accounts. As a result, Congress authorized NOW accounts for federally insured banks and savings and loans.

Today, we take for granted that computers make money market accounts, certificates of deposits, NOW checking accounts, and an endless array of mutual funds possible. But what it all comes down to is that there are only two ways to put your money to work: *as a lender or as an investor.*

A Lender Be

As Will Rogers said in the days of the Great Depression, "*I'm not so concerned about the return* on *my money as the return* of *my money.*" Many people still feel that way. Their first objective is to keep their money *safe.* Therefore, lenders are willing to accept lackluster interest returns of 4 percent or less in exchange for the assurance that their original investment will be returned intact. The only decisions they have to make are the length of the deposit term and the interest rate they'll accept.

When you deposit money in a savings account, you are *lending* money to a bank in exchange for interest income. After the Great Depression and scores of bank failures, many lenders felt they were walking on a financial high wire. To give them the safety they required, Congress established the Federal Deposit Insurance Corporation (FDIC) to protect up to $100,000 per account.

Banks and thrifts offer two basic instruments for earning interest income.

Money Market Accounts

Think of a money market account as a computerized passbook savings account. In the banking trade, they are called demand deposits. The main attraction is that you can make deposits and withdrawals any time you like. For this privilege you earn about 1 or 2 percent less interest than a fixed-term deposit. Money market mutual funds—while not federally insured—have had the same safety record as bank money market accounts, and they pay as much as 1 to 2 percent more interest than bank money market accounts.

Are money market accounts and passbook savings good for banks? You bet they are! Over the past two decades, the banking industry has been sustained by the profits from ultra-low-yielding savings accounts squirreled away by worried or uninformed lenders. The good news—not for lenders but for taxpayers—is that without these billions of dollars of low-interest money, the recent financial bailout of banks and savings and loans would have cost a great deal more.

Are money market accounts good for long-term investors? Probably not. Like millions of Americans, I started out with a passbook savings account. It held every penny of my entire wealth. My vision widened as I grew up and watched the numbers in my passbook increase. It turned out, however, that I would never get rich on 2 percent interest a year. I decided that when I had real money to invest I would put it to work in the stock market.

Fixed-Term Deposits

Insured certificates of deposit are term deposits. Terms are available from six months to as long as ten years. Like bonds, the longer the term, the higher the yield. Six-month insured CDs might yield 3 percent, but a five-year CD could yield well over 5 percent. To keep the money locked up inside the bank once you've made the deposit, the bank imposes a penalty for *early withdrawal.* The penalty is the loss of interest income for various periods, from ninety days to six months.

The problem with an insured CD is that if interest rates later rise, you are stuck with the lower yields until your CD matures, just as you would be with a bond. In your search for higher yields, you must withdraw the CD money and possibly pay the hefty early-withdrawal penalty. On the other hand, an insured certificate of deposit and money market account are the only interest-income investments where your principal is unaffected by changing interest rates. For example, if you deposit $1,000 in a one-year CD, you are assured of the return of the $1,000 one year later. With FDIC insurance, a bank failure along the way is no problem. Your money is safe. Or is it? In truth, the assured safe return of your money in the face of rising inflation puts your money at great risk. The shrinking dollar a lender gets back at the end of a CD term has less value in purchasing power than when it was invested in the first place.

Here's what I learned while talking to a farmer over a hay rake: If you earn only the inflation rate in interest, you can go directly to the poorhouse without passing go or collecting $100.

Let's say you deposit $10,000 in a one-year insured CD paying 4 percent interest. One year later, you'll get back $10,000, plus $400 interest, or a total of $10,400. However, the IRS does not love lenders. Each year the interest income you earn is taxed at your ordinary income tax rate. Let's say you're in a 28 percent federal and state tax bracket. The $400 of income can then shrink to $288, which leaves you with a net after-tax return of 2.9 percent. Now let say that over the past year inflation has risen 3 percent.

Here's how taxes and inflation can drain the real value out of your money:

Invest in a 4 percent insured CD	$10,000
One year later, with interest	$10,400
Less taxes @ 28 percent	$−112
Less inflation @ 3 percent	$−312
Purchasing power of the CD	$9,976

You may feel good about yourself; you might have a lot of ideas about how you'll spend your money in retirement. But the fact is that over the years, in terms of real purchasing power, your saving account resembles a highway truck stuck in the mud going nowhere.

If you want to preserve the future purchasing power of your money, you must earn a long-term return substantially higher than inflation and taxes.

That means dumping your low-yielding fixed savings accounts and investing in bonds, stocks, or equity mutual funds for their potential double-digit returns. What's that? You say you are scared to invest in the stock market?

The cold, hard fact is that you can't put your money to work without some risk.

- You can play it safe with a low-yielding federally insured savings account and risk losing out to rising inflation and taxes.
- You can reach out for higher yields with bonds and risk the possible loss of your principal.

Bond Basis Risk

If you've ever wondered why some people earn 3 percent in a money market account while others earn 7 percent on bonds, it's because the higher yields carry greater risks to principal if interest rates later rise. If you think this sounds a bit cold-blooded, you're right.

Over time savvy lenders, dissatisfied with the skimpy yields on money market accounts and certificates of deposit, have discovered that they can sometimes double their interest income with bonds or bond mutual funds. However, before you invest in a bond or bond fund, you need to know how bond basis risk can take a safe, guaranteed investment and turn it into a loss of principal. It's also important to understand that bond basis risk holds true for any bond—government, tax-exempt municipal, high yield junk, or blue-chip corporate bonds.

In other words, if you ever want to become a savvy investor on Wall Street, you must understand that changes in interest rates can change the market value of any bond or bond fund. Without this knowledge, you can get clobbered when interest rates rise.

Bond basis risk means that bond prices and yields move in opposite directions. Take a recent newspaper story about the bond market. "Treasury bond prices posted sharp gains today, with the price of 30-year Treasury bonds rising 25/32 point, or $7.81 per $1,000 face value, while its yield fell from 6.30 percent to 6.24 percent."

Here's the classic example of how bond basis risk can affect your original investment: Suppose that two years ago you purchased a $1,000 bond paying 7 percent. Now, two years later, you decide to sell your bond, but the current interest rate has risen to 8 percent. You call your broker and discover that your $1,000 bond is now worth only about $945. You are told that you have a discounted bond. Anyone who buys your bond, which is paying only 7 percent when current interest rates are 8 percent, will receive a discount so that their new investment in your 7 percent bonds will effectively earn 8 percent.

On the other hand, if interest rates have fallen to 6 percent after two years and you decide to sell your bond, you may be offered $1,055. You now have a premium bond, and a new buyer will pay the higher price to earn the bond's 7 percent yield when current rates are only 6 percent.

The degree of risk in bonds depends on how much interest rates move up or down *and* the maturity of the bond. The longer the maturity, the greater the risk of loss or gain. For example, a money market account has no bond basis risk because it keeps the maturities of its investments very short, often only sixty to ninety days, so that changes in interest rates do not affect its price. A dollar invested in a money market fund will always be worth a dollar, but a dollar invested in a five-year bond could lose about 4 percent of its market value if interest rates rise one full percentage point. That same one percentage point rate increase in a thirty-year bond, however, can reduce the market value of your bond by more than 11 percent.

When all the talk is about how much interest income you can earn, any bond fund that wants to attract investors' dollars reaches for the top yields. The only problem is that they rarely tell the investor that these funds can be very risky.

I'm always reminded of the lady who came up to me at a seminar and said, "Look here, Mr. Jorgensen, I invested $50,000 in some U.S. government bonds, but if I want to sell, they're worth only $46,000, and I can't afford to lose any money."

"Why did you invest in the bonds?" I asked in a soothing tone.

"Because the friendly financial planner at the bank told me that the government bonds were guaranteed and they were safe. Besides, I could earn two percent more interest on my money."

What he didn't tell her was the downside—that these higher-yielding bond funds carry greater risk as well as the potential for greater returns.

Bonds have an unseen danger.
Most people don't know about it,
and therefore it doesn't appear to exist.

High yields, however, are not the only factor to consider. *Total return,* which includes both bond price and yield, is a better measure of your investment's value. Total return is what you will earn at the end of the year, and it should include your interest income, plus or minus any changes in the market value of the bonds, and minus any sales charges and annual management fees.

The following table estimates total returns on bonds with varying maturities. As you can see, the longer the maturity, the greater the fluctuation in total return.

Changes in Total Return

	Interest Rate	Rates Remain Unchanged	Rates Go Up 1%	Rates Go Down 1%
Short-term				
3-year bond	4.5%	+4.6%	+2.7%	+6.5%
Intermediate-term				
10-year bond	6%	+6.1%	−0.6%	+13.4%
Long-term				
30-year bond	7%	+7.1%	−4.3%	+21.0%

SOURCE: *Fidelity Focus,* published by Fidelity Investments. Copyright 1993, FMR Corp. Reprinted with permission.

The main point: Investing in bonds and bond funds can be risky, and even the pros lose their shirts. For example, on a $1,000 30-year bond, if interest rates rise one full percentage point, the annual total return, *including the 7 percent interest* earned, less the reduced market value of the investment, could be a loss of $43. On the other hand, if interest rates fall three full percentage points as they did in the first half of 2001, you can make a lot of money investing in long-term bonds.

While you may shop for an insured certificate of deposit based on yield, don't shop for fixed-income bonds or bond funds the same way. Remember, you're entering the land of the unpredictable, where half of Wall Street is looking to boost the value of your investment, and the other half is looking for fire-sale prices. Also, don't ever come into the bond market with the idea that you've got it all figured out. One way to cut your losses or boost your profits in bonds is by understanding the degree of risk you take before you invest.

Money mangers say it's best to invest with maturities of about three to five years. Five years is where the yield curve tends to flatten out; after that, you run more risk than reward by grabbing the higher yields.

Smart investors keep bond maturities short.

Let me say again that millions of fixed-income investors will lose money in the years to come because they don't understand the risk they are taking on so-called safe and guaranteed long-term bonds or bond funds. They look at the high advertised yield, listen to the slick pitch from the broker or financial planner on how well they will do with their money, think about the guaranteed and safe bonds, grab the deal, and then lose their shirts.

How ridiculous can this whole scenario of investing long-term become? Consider the Mickey Mouse bonds issued by the Walt Disney Company. For the first time since 1954, an investor had the opportunity to buy 100-year bonds. Yielding barely one percentage point more than a 30-year bond, the market value of these bonds, with a maturity of one hundred years, could fall like a rock when interest rates rise.

How Safe Is *Safe*?

The major problem that bond investors encounter is that they don't fully understand the words *guarantee* and *safety* as applied to bonds. The guarantee stems from the fact that the bonds are unlikely to default. When you are told that a bond investment is "completely safe," it simply means that the bond issuer can be depended upon to pay the interest in a timely manner and the full face value of the bond at maturity. *Guarantee* and *safety,* however, say nothing about how the bond's market price will be adversely affected by rising interest rates.

Most people who invest in insured CDs believe that they are doing so without bond basis risk. The difference is that while the value of the CD always remains the purchase price, the CD could be worth less if you cash it in before maturity. The loss might be three months' or six months' worth of interest. If your account has not earned enough interest income when you make the withdrawal, the bank can dip into your principal to make up the difference. With bond income funds, you have no early withdrawal penalty; but to get your hands on your money you have to sell the fund at the current market price.

If all that sounds a bit crazy, you're right. Most lenders put their money to work by walking into a bank, opening an account, filling out the paperwork, writing a check, and taking what interest income they can get. It's easy. The financial institution does all the investing for you. But these turbulent times don't call for following in the footsteps of the past.

Increasingly, savvy lenders think in terms of objectives. If you want to earn interest income, the important points are *yield* and *safety.*

Like a savings account, a bond buyer is lending the borrower the money. The borrower agrees to pay the bondholder a certain rate of interest (the coupon rate) each year until the bond matures. At maturity, the borrower repays the bond's face value and the bond is retired.

Many borrowers issue two kinds of bonds: secured and unsecured. Secured bonds are backed by the borrower's assets, like a home mortgage loan or car loan. If the borrower can't make the payments, the lender can seize the collateral. Unsecured bonds are not backed by any particular asset. They are like a credit card debt on which you have promised to repay.

Bonds can also be insured and guaranteed by a bond insurance company. The coverage is underwritten by private insurers and guarantees both the timely payment of interest and the repayment of the bonds at maturity. Most of the bond insurance is written by two organizations: American Municipal Bond Assurance Corporation (AMBAC) and Municipal Bond Insurance Association (MBIA). If the issuer defaults on the principal or interest payments, these insurers step in and make the payments.

Before you invest in any bond or bond fund, find out whether the bonds are secured or unsecured, and if the future repayments are insured by a bond insurance company.

U.S. Inflation Savings Bonds (I-Bonds)

Every six months, on May 1 and November 1, the government sets the interest rate on these bonds based on a core interest rate and the inflation rate. However, as an added bonus, I-Bonds are free of state income tax. You can purchase I-Bonds from the Bureau of the Public Debt, or through most banks. They are sold in eight denominations ranging from $50 to $10,000. You must hold the bond for a minimum of six months or a maximum of thirty years. Like a CD, however, you must pay an early withdrawal penalty if you sell before you have owned the bonds for five years. The penalty is the loss of three months' interest.

FDIC Insured Bonds

Several financial firms have introduced a combination insured CD and long-term bond. Like a CD, these bonds are FDIC-insured up to $100,000 per individual. The bonds are not callable by the issuer at par (the purchase price) in the first year. However, like a regular bond with bond basis risk, you must understand that if you want your money before the bonds' maturity (usually ten or fifteen years) you have to sell them in the secondary market at the current market price, which could be much less than you paid. Some recent sales of these bonds after the first non-callable year have returned only about 75 percent of their original purchase price. However, the bonds are redeemable at par upon the death of the holder.

Money Market Funds

Bank money-market accounts and money-market mutual funds usually are invested in securities with an average maturity of between sixty and ninety days. The startling news is that do-it-yourself lenders can substantially increase their yields over a bank money-market account with essentially the same market safety. The short-term bond funds have an average annual maturity of around one to 5 years. These no-load funds typically earn as much as 2 percent more than a bank money market account with hardly any greater bond-basis market risk, and most funds have free check-writing privileges for amounts over $500.

Municipal Bonds

As they say on Monty Python, and now for something completely different: earning interest income without paying taxes. Some of the best opportunities for high net yields in recent years have been municipal bonds. States, cities, towns, water districts, school districts, highways, and even local hospitals all need to borrow money. When they do, they offer lenders interest income that is free of most income taxes. But not all income is tax-free. If the fund pays out realized capital gains, those payouts are fully taxable.

Municipal bonds, known as munis, come in several different forms, depending on the risk rating of their interest payments and the repayment at maturity. There are two major types of municipal bonds:

- **General Obligation Bonds (GOs).** These bonds are the safest tax-free bonds you can buy because the payments for interest and principal come from general tax revenues. Agencies that issue GOs can raise taxes, if necessary, to pay bondholders.
- **Revenue Bonds (REVs).** These bonds are issued for a specific project such as construction of a bridge, a power plant, a hospi-

tal, or housing project. The income to pay the bondholders is expected to come from the revenues generated by the specific project. The risk is that if the income from the project fails to generate enough money to pay interest or pay off the bonds, the bonds can default. Although this is rare, defaults do happen. The Washington Public Power Supply System, which became known as "WOOPS," defaulted on $2.25 billion of revenue bonds because the nuclear power plants they financed—which were to generate electric power—were never built. This was the largest default in history, and it told investors that one of the risks involved with revenue bonds is political risk.

Bond Anticipation Notes (BANs)

These municipal bonds are issued as short-term notes with repayment expected to come from the proceeds of an upcoming bond issue yet to be sold. Tax anticipation notes (TANs) are short-term notes similar to BANs, with repayment expected from tax revenues.

How to Compute Equivalent Yields

If you invest in municipal bonds, it helps to understand *tax-equivalent yields.* Let me put it this way: Municipal bond funds could pay 5 percent tax-free. To earn this much tax-free you might have to find a bank offering an insured CD at 6.9 percent. In other words, if you could earn almost 7 percent at the bank or mutual fund, and pay your income taxes at 28 percent, your after-tax return would be about 5 percent!

To calculate the value of your current taxable yield compared to a muni's yield, take your current tax rate, written as a decimal, and subtract it from 1.00. If your marginal tax rate is 28 percent, subtract .28 from 1.00 and get .72. If the tax-free bond fund is yielding 5 percent, divide 5 by .72 and get 6.94 percent, the tax-equivalent yield you need to equal the municipal bond's tax-free yield of 5 percent.

If you live in a state like California, with hefty state income tax rates, your combined tax rate might be 37 percent (28 percent federal and 9 percent state). Your calculations would be 1.00 minus .37, or .63. Divide the 5 percent tax-free yield by .63 and you'll need to earn a taxable yield of 7.93 percent to match the 5 percent tax-free yield.

If you invest in municipal bond mutual funds and you live in a state with state income taxes, it's important to consider double-tax-free municipal bond funds. These so-called single-state mutual funds can invest in bonds issued in your state, so the income generally qualifies for both federal and state tax exemption. If you live in a state without state income taxes, you can shop for nationwide municipal bond funds. As you can see, earning interest income has become so goofy that you can often turn to the government's I-Bonds or the state and city municipal bonds and earn more spendable cash than you might through any bank or broker.

Zero Coupon Bonds

Zero coupon bonds get their name from the fact that bond certificates once came with interest coupons attached to the bond for interest payment. These were called *bearer bonds,* because they were considered the property of anyone who held them. Zero coupon bonds don't pay interest each year, so they in effect have no coupons.

Zero coupon bonds are sold at a discount from face value and return to the investor the full amount of the bond at maturity. They work just like U.S. savings bonds that cost $25 and return $50 at maturity. You can buy zeros for almost any length of time.

For a long-term zero (about twenty years), you might pay just $250 for a $1,000 bond; for shorter maturities (about five years), you might pay $750 for the same bond.

However, zeros do earn interest income—the difference between the purchase price and face of the bond—and this imputed interest is treated by the Internal Revenue Service as ordinary income each year as it is imputed to your account. Many people don't like paying taxes on interest income they don't actually receive each year, so brokers suggest you put the zeros in your IRA or other retirement plans where taxes are deferred until you take out the money.

Zero coupon bonds are a "hands-off" investment. You can buy a fifteen-year zero bond, pay your taxes each year, and collect the full face value of the bond fifteen years later. What you are gambling on is that during this period interest rates won't change, because with long-term zero coupon bonds, the price can skyrocket with falling interest rates; but with rising interest rates the share price can plunge, making many people feel like they're sitting in a deck chair on the *Titanic.*

Why do people buy zero coupon bonds? Because they sound so simple, because they can fill a need—like saving for college expenses sixteen years from today—and because they are very profitable for brokers and financial planners to sell. Once again, the suits that run around Wall Street have been able to fashion zero coupon bonds from a wide array of bonds. There are tax-free zeros, corporate zeros, and Treasury zeros (sometimes known as TIGRs, CATS, and STRIPS). The banks, not to be left out, offer federally insured zero coupon certificates of deposit.

Ginnie Mae Bonds

Over the years many individual investors have turned to mortgage-backed securities as a way to boost yields. The most popular investment is Ginnie Mae bond funds. Ginnie Mae bonds are named after the government agency that issues them, the Government National Mortgage Association (GNMA).

Here's how Ginnie Mae are created: A homeowner obtains a mortgage to buy a new home. The mortgage lender then sells the mortgage to GNMA to obtain money to make more loans. GNMA packages the loans and sells them to security firms, who offer them to the public in the form of a mutual fund.

Ginnie Maes work differently from all other bonds. As homeowners repay their mortgages each month, the investor receives both a return of principal and interest income. Consequently, if you hold a Ginnie Mae bond to maturity, you'll end up with a zero-value bond. With regular bonds, your principal is repaid at maturity, when you sell or when the bond is called. With a Ginnie Mae mutual fund you can automatically reinvest both the return of principal and interest income, receive both in cash or a combination of each.

Ginnie Mae bond funds are often sold on the pretext that they are safe from default because they are backed by a government agency. That is true, but they are not safe from bond basis risk that can change the market value of the fund's share price at any time. Although Ginnie Maes usually have yields much higher than insured CDs, there is a danger for the investor if interest rates change. That's because Ginnie Mae funds can be made up of mortgages with relatively high interest rates. If rates fall, mortgages may be refinanced early, lowering the fund's yield. If interest rates rise, however, homeowners won't refinance and yields may lag the market. If you are thinking about investing in Ginnie Maes because of their current yield, you should also think about total return and carefully consider the volatility of the share price.

Shopping for a Bond Fund

Cutting through the confusion about yield and bond risk is not easy. Mutual funds tout the best numbers they can find. When they've earned good returns in the past, they don't hesitate to put those numbers in the headlines of their advertisements. Here's a checklist to help you get through the minefield of buzzwords.

SEC Yield

This is the Securities and Exchange Commission's way of quantifying the so-called thirty-day yield, minus fund expenses. It starts with the fund's income per share over the preceding thirty days, minus expenses, and adjusts for the market value of the bonds in the portfolio and other income. The results are divided by the fund's share price and annualized. It is the most reliable comparison between funds.

12-Month Average Yield

This represents the fund's per-share income during the past twelve months divided by the share price adjusted for capital gains. It only tells what you could have earned over the past year. If a twelve-month yield in an ad looks like it could pay for a spending spree through Monte Carlo, don't bank on it. Past returns are no guarantee of future payouts after you invest.

Total Return

Total return can be the most misleading number of all. Total return is calculated as if all dividends during the period are reinvested (whether they were or not); account for the fund's sales commissions and include all capital gains or losses. If interest rates have fallen in the past year, a bond fund's total return will be displayed in big letters in the ad. That's because falling interest rates, as we've already learned, can boost capital gains and total returns.

What all these numbers can mean to a new investor is best described by a recent newspaper advertisement for a bond fund offered by a bank. It boasted a current yield of 6.6 percent when most savings deposits were paying around 5 percent. The fund sounded a lot better than an insured CD. In even bigger print, the ad told the would-be investor that the average total return for the most recent year was 7.53 percent, and over five years a hefty 8.98 percent.

But anyone who grabbed a magnifying glass and looked at the fine print found a different story. The years used to compute total return were a period when interest rates in general were falling, increasing capital gains profits substantially. Also, the bond fund had a 4 percent front-end sales commission, so investors in the first year could end up with lower returns than the low-yielding CDs they were leaving. What's more, if interest rates were to rise during the following year on these longer-term bond funds, the actual return could be much less than might be expected from the flashy ad, and it could even be a loss.

For example, a $10,000 investment paying 6.6 percent at year's end should have earned $660 in interest and be worth $10,660. However, with an up-front sales commission of 4 percent, the actual net investment would be only $9,600. At year's end, with interest income on that lower amount, the total would be only $10,233. Alternatively, to put it another way, that's a 2.3 percent return on your original investment, not the 6.6 percent highlighted in the ads.

However, it gets worse. If rates rise one percentage point during the year, the total return could actually decline. That's because the market value of the bond fund could fall $50 per $1,000 of face value. In this example, on the $10,000 initial investment with a 4 percent commission, the year-end total return could actually be:

Initial investment	$9,600
Interest income of	$633
A capital loss	$500
A market value of	$9,733

Again, under this example, the hard cold fact is that if you sold this bond fund after one year, you'd take a loss of $267 on your original $10,000 investment.

With a strongbox filled with bonds and fixed-saving accounts, you can be riding shotgun on a stagecoach going backward in time.

For most investors who want to build wealth and retirement security over time, lending money just can't do the job. I learned that from the farmers; now you can learn this from me. Chances are, after taxes and inflation you won't even have the purchasing power your money had when you first invested it.

From talking to thousands of longtime bank savers who lack confidence in the stock market, I realize it will take courage for them to change the way they put their extra money to work. I hope you have that courage to change from a lender to an investor, just as I did.

STEP 3

Kill Those Credit Cards

You'll never get rich paying off credit cards.

Admit it. You have a wallet or purse crammed with credit cards, gas station cards, grocery store cards, frequent flier cards, and even some cards you haven't touched in more than a year. Well, you've got to give the people who issue the charge cards credit. They can tempt anyone to buy now and pay later. And once you're hooked on plastic, they know how to slap on fees, penalties, and sky-high interest rates. They'll even charge you a service fee for the privilege of keeping your credit card firmly planted in your purse or wallet!

There are now more than a billion credit cards in circulation nationwide—almost four cards for every American citizen—and credit card debt during the plastic prosperity of the 1990s soared to triple the debt of a decade earlier. Today, cardholders pay an average of $800 in interest a year, or a total of $43 billion. To reap big profits on this spending spree, credit card issuers have kept the average credit card interest rate above 18 percent.

The credit card industry started in 1950 when Diner's Club issued the first credit card that could be used at different businesses in New York City. Between 1950 and the early 1960s, bank cards could only be used locally or statewide. In 1966, California's Bank of America offered the first nationwide credit card, Bank Americard (now Visa), by forming a network of banks in numerous states. Other banks quickly formed a competing network, known as MasterCard.

But perhaps the biggest change in nationwide credit cards occurred in 1996, when the U.S. Supreme Court ruled that state laws that restricted fees and other charges for residents were superseded by federal law. That ruling opened the floodgates by allowing any card issuer to use nationwide the laws in effect in the state of issue. As a result, the major card issuers raced to set up shop in South Dakota, Arizona, and Delaware, where state laws permit almost any fees and charges.

As a result, Americans now find credit card solicitations cramming their mailboxes as new players try to steal customers from other credit card issuers. The offers come with low "teaser" interest rates, no annual fees the first year, and an array of discounts, points, coupons, and credits on future purchases. One airline even offered a coupon for a free round-trip companion ticket anywhere the airline flies in the United States when the customer signed up for its credit card. But the bargain cards often turn out to be more illusion than reality. Many card issuers seeking to poach customers from their competitors ultimately reject about half the applications.

Unless you live under a rock, you're probably aware that some of America's biggest non-bank companies, such as AT&T, General Motors, Ford, American Airlines, and General Electric are elbowing one another for a piece of the credit card business. The reason, as Willie Sutton once said about banks, is *that's where the money is.* Credit card issuers make billions of dollars in profits a year, and with this kind of money pumping up the bottom line, department stores, gasoline companies, supermarkets, and other retailers want a bigger piece of the action. They are rushing to join the banks and big corporations with their own Visas or MasterCards. Kroger, the big Cincinnati-based grocery chain, offers MasterCards to its customers, and Nordstrom, the Seattle-based department store chain, issues its own card. Shell Oil Company can make your gasoline credit card a MasterCard. Not only will you be able to buy gas, but you can shop till you drop at the local department store. "The only credit card you'll need," says Shell.

Within the credit card industry, retailer cards are referred to as co-branded cards. Because retailers are interested in attracting customers to their own stores, the co-branded cards are expected to be more competitive than typical bank cards. Shell Oil allows drivers to save money at the pump and receive rebates on other purchases. What's important to understand is that credit card companies don't make a profit on what you buy; they make a profit on what you don't pay back each month.

But today, credit card companies see more and more consumers grabbing home-equity loans at half the interest rates of credit cards and deducting the payments, while the number of interest-paying customers shrink. In 1999, 44 percent of consumers paid bills in full compared with 29 percent in 1991. The result is that card issuers have been hit with a double whammy: They must now depend on fees and high interest rates to make a profit.

Sneaky Tricks

To squeeze the cardholders that pay over time, the card companies have developed an array of sneaky tricks:

Change the Terms and Conditions

One sneaky trick is to frequently change the terms and conditions of your credit card agreement. Card issuers are required to give you notice (typically fifteen days) before increasing your interest rate, lowering your credit limit, adding fees and penalties, reducing or eliminating the grace period, or cutting back on bonus programs. But if you don't read through what appears to be junk mail carefully, you may easily miss seeing these notices and you can end up paying a lot more than you expected for the use of your cards.

The Check Is in the Mail

It's tempting, for example, to cash that $10,000 check made payable to you that came in the mail. But if you do, the low *teaser* interest rate can quickly vanish and the $10,000 is added to your current monthly balance. You will be socked with 18 percent or even higher interest on your entire debt (including your monthly charges) until you pay off the loan *and your monthly charges in full.* You're stuck with rates often twice those for home-equity loans, and your credit card interest is not tax-deductible.

Late Payments

Now we come to the real bandits at work. Credit card issuers have developed an enormously profitable *late payment* business by making it more difficult for cardholders to pay on time and gouging them with fees and penalty interest rates. A survey of 95 credit card offers found the average grace period for making payments without paying interest had dropped to 22.5 days from a longtime standard of thirty days. However, that's only half the story. The grace period usually begins when the card statement is printed and mailed, not when you receive it. Most cardholders typically have about 15 days to make the payment in full to escape fees and higher interest rates. The problem for millions of cardholders is that the *credit card company* determines when your payment was received on time. It's not when you mailed the payment, it's whatever the credit card company says it posted it to your account.

Let's say the card issuer receives your payment after the due date. Today, you can expect a late fee of almost $30. Then expect the credit card company to trigger a new penalty interest rate on the entire previous month's balance. A typical penalty rate was 22.9 percent a year, or 6 points more than payments received on time. Some card issuers have recently jacked up the penalty interest rate to 27.5 percent. This rate applies to a cardholder that makes a late payment, exceeds a credit limit, or has the account closed.

Don't expect much help climbing off these rates. After you make six on-time monthly payments, your rate can drop by one percentage point! Worse yet, the card issuer doesn't send you a special notice if it starts charging the punitive rate. You were warned about this when you first applied for the card. And for most folks, with the late payments on their record, they may not be able to switch credit cards and obtain a lower rate.

The "key" to gouging the cardholder is the company's control over determining when your payment is late. It now turns out that several card issuers didn't play fair. In August 2000, Citigroup's Citibank agreed to pay $45 million to settle early payment claims. Then in September 2000, Chase Manhattan agreed to pay $22 million to settle consumer lawsuits alleging credit card customers were forced to pay extra interest and late fees even when monthly payments arrived on time. The fine print in your credit card agreement usually says "A payment is officially late even if you sent it in on time but it got held up in the mail." In reality, it often depends on holidays, mail delays, and the time your payment sits in the credit card office waiting to be posted to the computer. It doesn't take a rocket scientist to figure out that an understaffed office can make a lot of money on late fees for a credit card company.

Your friendly credit card company also wants to you know that it might punish you even if you've always paid your card balance on time. In search of fee income, some card issuers even check your credit report to see if you paid any other card or account late. If so, they can rate you a higher risk and slap on the almost 30 percent rates. And if you underpay—even by $1—you could be charged interest on the full amount of the balance to the date of the statement.

Balance Transfer Fees

Almost every day a bunch of offers to transfer your old credit card balance to a new credit card fall out of your mailbox. What you may not realize is that some card issuers are tacking on a fee of 3 percent, with a maximum of $29, to let the money go. When you cancel your card and don't pay off the balance, several credit cards charge you as much as 26.99% interest on the remaining balance. If you cancel a credit card, make sure you've paid it off first to avoid all the fees and sky-high interest rates.

Cash Advance Fees

You are on the road and you need money. You tap your credit card's available balance, slip the cash into your pocket, and take off. There is only one problem. The typical advance fee can be from 3 to 5 percent of the amount you received and interest starts the moment you get the cash.

Teaser Rates

Because almost everyone who wants a credit card already has one, one way for card issuers to drum up new business is to offer special deals to new applicants. The competition is so fierce that in May 2001 several card issuers offered a 0 percent introductory rate good for as long as six months. Many of these deals apply only to new purchases, but some to balance transfer.

To check out the special offers of dozens of cards, find low rate cards, and what's the best card for you with excellent or poor credit, log onto www.creditcardfreedom.com.

For the most part, these big marketing promotions pay off for the card issuers. If you carry a balance and pay interest each month, the card issuers are making a clever gamble that you'll believe the low teaser interest rate in the advertisements will last forever. When the high interest rates kick in, the card issuer is also betting that it won't induce you to find a lower-rate card. For the most part, card issuers have been proven right.

A Trip to Nowhere

Now let's see how paying these high credit card interest rates can flatten your financial future like a herd of overweight elephants stomping through a muddy riverbank. Credit card debt can, in effect, pound the life out of your financial health.

You run up a $2,000 balance on your credit card. (The average cardholder who regularly carries a monthly balance has a debt of $4,200 spread over roughly six credit cards.) Now let's say you decide not to charge on the card again until you pay off the balance. The minimum monthly payment, around 2 percent of the balance, is about $40 a month. Of that amount, $33.13 will go for interest expense on a card with a 19.8 percent rate, and only $6.67 to reduce your outstanding balance. At the end of the first year, if you send in only the minimum amount required each month, your $2,000 debt will be reduced by just $100! The card issuers are feeding at the trough, while cardholders are on a crash diet.

And it gets worse. If you continue to send in the minimum amount each month and don't make any more charges, you'll be paying off the original $2,000 debt for the next 31 years! By the time you make the final payment, it will have cost you $7,126 to pay off a $2,000 balance. When people realize how credit card interest payments can send their financial security up in flames, they often visualize the bank manager who issued the card standing there holding the matchbook and gasoline can and grinning. To paraphrase Ross Perot, that big sucking sound you hear is your money draining from your wallet to your banker's bottom line.

Financial freedom starts with a zero balance.

While credit card holders are getting clobbered, the card issuers are offering fancy extras to persuade more consumers to keep high monthly balances on the books for as long as possible. In order to make it even easier for you to run up more debt—and pay more interest—many credit card issuers have reduced the required minimum monthly payments. One credit card company now has a minimum monthly payment as low as 1.67 percent of the monthly balance on its gold card. Some issuers will even let you skip a payment, and keep paying the interest until you expire.

The rich rewards are for the nimble and courageous shopper, because if you increase your minimum payment under this example from $40 a month to only $70 a month, you can cut the repayment schedule from 31 years to just 39 months! If you add as little as 25 cents a day, or $7.50 a month, to your monthly payment, you can save as much as $5,000 in interest! You'll move a big chunk of the bank's bottom line to your own simply by paying an extra two bits a day.

It should also come as no surprise that people who pay off their balance in full each month get the best deal. They get what amounts to a free card (minus the annual fees) and a float on their money before they pay off their card balance. The credit card issuers hate these people; they are forced to make their money from the 56 percent of consumers who typically carry a revolving balance each month.

Let's compare what happens to someone who carries an average monthly balance of $4,200 with someone who pays off his or her monthly balance in full each month. Assuming an interest rate of 18.9 percent, you've saved about $800 a year if you pay off your balance in full each month. In addition, since you would have paid taxes on the interest payments, and assuming you're in a 30 percent tax bracket, you'd need to have earned about $1,150 a year before taxes just to pay the carrying cost with the same monthly balance all year. Now, let's assume you put that $1,150 in an IRA each year. Instead of being robbed by a credit card issuer, you can use the magic of compounded growth to build your retirement nest egg.

Let's say you have twenty years left until retirement and each year you can put the same amount of money you might otherwise spend on credit card interest into your IRA. Earning last decade's average stock market return, you could accumulate $135,000 in twenty years. If you started saving and investing this money at age 35, and made these same investments each year to age 65, your nest egg would be Fort Knox. The value of the IRA could now be well over half a million! If you've learned nothing else, remember there is no better financial move than paying off credit card debt and socking the money you would have paid in interest into your IRA. I learned this from the farmers who paid cash for everything. This helped me withstand the rain of credit card offers I got when started working after college, and it turned the *pay off the balance each month* plan into a major part of my financial security.

Remember that the pile of cash I accumulated came from the interest and the taxes I would otherwise have paid on my credit card debt. For more help in learning about credit card fees, interest rates, late payments, and other charges, log onto the American Bankers Association's website, www.aba.com, or www.truthaboutcredit.org.

The Best Credit Cards

The Payoff Card

If you intend to pay off the balance in full each month within the grace period, you don't care what the interest rate is because you won't be incurring any. Some of the high-interest-rate cards offer the best deal to those who pay off their balance in full each month.

The Credit Balance Card

The key element to look for in a card where you intend to carry a credit balance is a low interest rate. Most of the low-interest-rate cards today have a variable rate tied to the prime rate plus a fixed premium. Like an adjustable-rate mortgage, the interest rate on your credit card balance can change as interest rates raise or fall.

Methods of Interest Calculation

There are four basic ways that credit card companies can figure the interest charges on your outstanding balance. From best to worst, they are:

1. average daily balance, excluding new purchases
2. two-cycle average daily balance, excluding new purchases
3. average daily balance, including new purchases
4. two-cycle average daily balance, including new purchases

Most card issuers figure interest charges on a one-month period. The amount outstanding each day is totaled and divided by the number of days in the month to get the average daily balance. Here's how the two-cycle method works, according to Robert McKinley of RAM Research: "Say your previous balance was zero and you charge a $1,000 purchase on January 1. When your January statement arrives in February, you can either pay the balance off in full, thus avoiding interest charges, or make a partial payment and incur interest. If you decide to pay less than the full balance, you will be assessed interest (on your February statement) from January 1. Under the one-cycle method, card issuers assess interest only for February." The two-cycle method can be quite deceiving, so consider this: Theoretically, a cardholder paying off the full balance every third month could incur up to four extra months of interest per year.

It should come as no surprise that the card issuer can make substantially more interest income on the same credit card debt depending on the way interest is calculated. Here's an example of a shopper who charged $1,000 the first month, paid the minimum amount due, charged another $1,000 the next month, and paid the entire balance. The cardholder repeated this pattern three more times during the year.

Interest Rate	**12%**	**17.3%**	**19.8%**
Average daily balance, excluding new purchases	$40.00	$57.60	$66.00
Average daily balance, including new purchases	$80.00	$115.20	$132.00
Two-cycle average daily balance, including new purchases	$120.00	$172.80	$198.00

SOURCE: Reprinted by permission of Bankcard Holders of America.

Here's a list of the tricks card issuers can use to boost your interest expense on outstanding balances.

Start the interest clock

A growing number of credit cards start charging interest on credit balances the date you make the purchases—in many cases, even before you leave the store!

Use compound interest
Some card issuers now use daily compounding of interest instead of monthly compounding. This means that interest is calculated and added to your balance daily instead of monthly.

Use time-tiered rates
Some card issuers have introduced an interest rate gimmick called a time-tiered rate. Current purchases, including those made in the previous month, are charged a lower rate, while purchases that are more than two billing cycles old are charged a much higher rate.

The Debit Card

This card works in reverse of a credit card: You pay cash for each purchase. The card usually deducts your purchase from your checking account immediately. You may also (as with an ATM card) get cash back from the merchant.

But before you rush out and grab a debit card to replace your credit card, consider this: Credit cards carry some legal protections that debit cards don't, such as dispute resolution if an item you purchase is defective. The credit card agreement gives you the right to withhold payments until the problem is fixed. With a debit card, by the time you discover the product's deficiencies the merchant has your money.

Hotels, rental-car companies, and even gas stations can put a hold on a customer's debit card to insure that there's enough money to cover the bill. This can create a problem if you use a debit card without a large balance in your checking account. Many of your outstanding checks could bounce before the hold is lifted, or you could be prevented from withdrawing money from your checking account.

If someone steals your credit card, the most you're liable for is

$50. But if you lose or someone cops your debit card, you can't be held liable for losses only as long as you report the theft *before* any money has been taken from your checking account. If you report the theft within two days, you're only liable for $50. The next deadline is within sixty days of the loss. Thereafter, the bank isn't required to reimburse you for any losses.

The problem is that often consumers don't know their debit card has been stolen until their checks bounce, or until they get calls from angry merchants over unpaid bills. Banks have also launched marketing campaigns to offer debit card customers points to redeem for merchandise and U.S. airfares. But many banks link rewards programs to debit card transactions that don't require a PIN. That's because banks make about half as much money from the merchant with a PIN-based debit card transaction. If you use a debit card, make sure your purchase is based on a PIN for your safety and the ability to continue to get cash back when you make a purchase.

How to Reduce Credit Card Debt

The best way to cut your credit card debt is to simply go "cold turkey" and cancel your cards. If you can't wean yourself altogether, at least reduce the number of cards you carry to one or two. Following are a few suggestions to help you use your cards wisely.

- Charge only what you can repay at month's end. People often ask me how to boost their savings account yield at the bank, yet these same people are often paying 17 or 18 percent interest on their credit-card debt. That's the kind of activity that can kill your plans to get rich.
- Pay off revolving charge card balances as soon as possible. If you can, take some of your low-yielding savings and pay off your

credit card debt now. If you have paid off a department store card on which you were paying $50 a month, apply that $50 to another credit card balance. Do that until you pay off all your credit cards. If you can't make these payments, use some of the money you pay yourself first before you invest.

One suggestion for cutting impulse spending comes from the Institute of Consumer Financial Education (ICFE), a nonprofit organization dedicated to helping people do a better job of spending and saving their money. ICFE says that people need to practice safe spending. To help, they offer a credit card condom, which slips over the card and carries a warning to the overextended user. "Keep this condom cover over your credit card. The few seconds it takes to get the card ready for use can reduce the urge to spend, spend, spend, and then you'll have money to invest." (For more information about the Institute of Consumer Financial Education, the web address is www.icfe.info. You can also write Box 34070, San Diego, CA 92163, or call 619-232-8811.)

If You Get Sick and Can't Work

Credit card companies offer a credit protection plan, and you are guaranteed enrollment! The plan pays the minimum monthly amount due on your credit card bill (often only two percent of the total bill) if you are unable to work because of involuntary unemployment, illness, or accident. The payments continue for up to one full year or until you go back to work, whichever comes first. In the event of death, the plan will pay off the entire card balance up to $5,000. That may sound like a good idea until you look at the cost of an extra 2 percent a month based on your outstanding card balance. This is very expensive disability and life insurance protection, which you can avoid with your own adequate insurance policies.

If You Lose Your Credit Card

If your cards are lost or stolen, be sure to call the credit card issuers immediately. Most credit card companies have a 24-hour hotline number for reporting missing cards. Once you report the missing cards, the law says you have no further liability, and your maximum out-of-pocket liability is $50 per card for unauthorized charges. Most card issuers can give you a new number in minutes. It is a good idea to follow up your phone call with a letter to the credit card company sent by certified mail.

Credit Card Fraud

Any time you make a remote transaction, you are at risk of credit card fraud.

Identity theft has become the nation's fastest-growing white-collar crime. In 2002, more than 45,000 Americans were victims of identity theft; about half the thefts involved credit card fraud.

The shocking fact today is that a thief armed with a debit card number can go on a shopping spree and drain your bank account within hours. You are then faced with bounced checks all over town and a fight with your bank to prove you never used the card in the first place. Or, the thief can steal your Social Security number and date of birth, open an instant credit account at a store, and walk out with five thousand dollars' worth of merchandise in your name.

The important point to remember is that the crooks don't need someone's credit card to steal money. In 2001 nearly 10 percent of Americans were struck with unauthorized purchases on their ATM, debit, or credit card, and this number is expected to grow again next year and possibly top 15 percent by year's end.

The old warning was: ***never let the card out of your sight.*** But many cardholders whose cards have been used without their permission never lost their plastic. Their card numbers may have been copied by a store clerk during a transaction, thieves might have plucked the numbers from a garbage can or dumpster, hackers may have found the data bases on a website that sells credit card numbers, or some bank or online company may have sold the card numbers.

Skimming

The fastest growing way to steal credit card data is by *skimming* them off a genuine card. The magnetic stripe on a card's back is encoded with a cardholder's name, account number, expiration date, and a security code—everything a crook needs to start using the card. And today it's easy to read the once unreadable magnetic stripe. Thieves simply buy small, unobtrusive magnetic stripe readers over the Internet and alter them to record all of the data on a card's magnetic stripe with a mere swipe of the card. Dishonest waiters or department store clerks can simply take your credit card and run it through a stripe reader concealed in their pocket or purse while they have your card to ring up a legitimate purchase.

Fraud Clusters

The latest development is *identity fraud clusters.* For example, teachers within the Los Angeles Unified School District suddenly began receiving harassing phone calls from bill collectors. This can occur when a thief has your personal information and obtains *instant credit* in your name at an electronic or warehouse store. The Los Angeles schoolteachers got their credit card statements and found that charges had been made in their names at half the merchants in a nearby town. Investigators believe that an employee within the school district may have compiled a list of the teachers' names, Social Security numbers, and other personal information, and sold it. In this way an unhappy employee or one who is simply in desperate need of cash can pose a real risk to the financial well-being of his or her co-workers.

Or consider this. Thieves buy tens of thousands of credit card numbers from a bank or other information vendor and bill you $19.95 for nonexistent Internet services. It's easy to overlook transaction of less than twenty dollars buried in your card statement, but the thieves can rake in hundreds of millions of dollars a month for a service that does not exist.

Here are a few precautions that might help you avoid the inconvenience of straightening out your credit card account later:

- Keep your credit cards concealed. If you leave them out in the open, scam operators can copy the numbers and use your card. Thieves can also sell your telephone card number to people who make long distance calls around the world. Keep the card hidden when you make a phone call in public.
- Keep the carbon copies from purchase charges and cash advances. A carbon copy of your receipt is as good as the credit card itself to a crook. Do not give out your credit card number and expiration date over the phone or use it on a website that is not secure. Don't ever accept the offer of a free trip or prizes if you first show "good faith" by making a payment on your card.
- Destroy all cards you no longer use. Then be sure to notify your credit bureau that you no longer have the account. While these accounts are open, they allow you to receive credit and potentially run up a lot of debt. This is not a good sign to someone who is considering offering you credit.

Fraud Alarm

It's important to carefully review your monthly credit card statement. This may be your first hint that someone has made unauthorized purchases on your card. If you have a debit card, you may be overdrawn at the bank before you even know you have been hit by fraud. While federal law limits a cardholder's liability to $50, card issuers won't reimburse you for the time and expense of repairing a damaged credit history, a job that can take months or sometimes years of effort and repeated phone calls.

In addition, excess charges and late payments on accounts you never opened can create a problem with your credit report that could hold up approval of a car loan or a pending mortgage. The three big credit reporting agencies—Equifax, Experian, and Trans Union—have a daily credit monitoring service that will immediately alert you by e-mail whenever an inquiry is made on your credit file or a new account is opened in your name. The cost is about $40 a year.

Credit Bureau Reports

It's important to review your credit bureau file every year. In addition to outright fraud, there are other common errors and potential problems consumers face in maintaining good credit histories.

Mistaken Identities

All three reporting agencies rely chiefly on Social Security numbers to verify that information is entered on the correct report. But with this number as the only identifier, the potential for errors is huge. This happened to me once when I was denied credit supposedly because of a bad credit record. When I went over the report, (which was in my identical name), I found the report was not mine. Someone else had used my Social Security number.

Misapplied Charges

Errors frequently occur because charges, loans, or debts are attributed to the wrong person. You must be careful that only *your* records are on your report.

Uncorrected Errors

You can complain about mistakes, but it's often another matter to correct your credit bureau report. The Fair Credit Reporting Act entitles consumers to contest mistakes on their credit records and to have them promptly corrected. When a challenge is filed by a consumer (in the case of fraud, you might file the corrections for each unauthorized charge), a credit bureau is required to complete an investigation and amend the report as required within thirty days. The cardholder is supposed to receive a corrected copy of his or her report without charge not more than five days later.

That's the way it's supposed to work. In practice, however, you will have to continue to make inquiries and review your credit report until the problems are corrected. You should also understand that a credit bureau report lists only the charges and other information received from the merchant that originally made the charge. You cannot change the report yourself. Therefore, you should inform both the credit bureau and the creditor who put the charges on your report, in writing. Then send this to all three bureaus with your request to change your credit reports.

What Can You Do?

You should obtain a copy of your credit bureau report each year from all three credit reporting companies (they often don't have the same information on their reports). Check everything over carefully. Make certain your name, place of birth, date of birth, and other individual items are correct.

In most states, you'll pay $8.50 (plus tax) for a report from each bureau. You are entitled to a free copy if you are turned down for a loan, or if you challenge charges on what you believe are mistakes on your report. In most cases, you must request a copy of your free report within sixty days of any denial of credit.

You can contact the three bureaus by phone, in writing, or by using their web sites. Reports by e-mail can arrive within a few-minutes, by phone within seven days, and by mail in 13 days. Here's the contact information for each credit bureau:

- Equifax: Phone: 1-800-685-1111; Website: www.equifax.com; Address: Equifax, P.O. Box 740241, Atlanta, GA 30374.
- Experian: Phone: 1-800-392-1122; Website: www.experian.com; Address: Experian, P.O. Box 2002, Allen, TX 75013.
- Trans Union: Phone: 1-800-888-4213; Website: www.transunion.com; Address: Trans Union, P.O. Box 1000, Chester, PA 19022.

How to Find the Best Deal on a Credit Card

A good source for learning about credit cards and finding the best credit card is RAM Research. It has monitored credit cards since 1986. It tracks credit card fees and interest rates and publishes a monthly CardTrak newsletter that lists hundreds of current credit cards with information on how to find the best one. RAM Research also has a list of secured credit card programs. The newsletter is $5 a copy from RAM Research, Box 1700, Frederick, MD 21702, 800-344-7714. Or go online at www.cardtrak.com. You can also check out the best credit card deals with www.bankrate.com and www.cardweb.com.

If You Can't Get a Credit Card

If you have a bad credit history and are now working your way out of debt, or if you have insufficient credit history, the major credit card issuers may turn down your application for a new card. A great way to rebuild your credit and flash a Visa or MasterCard is to obtain a *secured credit card.* Even if your credit history shows liens, charge-offs, repossessions, or bankruptcy, as long as your problems are under control and in the past, you are likely to qualify for a secured credit card.

To obtain a secured credit card you have to establish a savings account with the bank. If you don't pay your bills, the bank can use the money in the savings account to meet the credit card payments. For example, the minimum savings deposit can range from $500 to $2,500 depending on what credit line you want. Depending on the issuer and your credit history, the credit line can vary from 50 percent to 150 percent of your deposit. Most issuers of secured credit cards will pay interest on your savings account, but some pay only the passbook savings rate. Most secured cards charge higher interest rates and higher annual fees than unsecured cards, and a one-time application fee is often charged.

A secured Visa or MasterCard looks and works just like any other credit card. It is simply a bank credit card guaranteed by a savings deposit. If you want to apply for a secured credit card, deal only with a bank. Don't fall for the newspaper and magazine ads that guarantee to find you a credit card, no matter what your credit history, for an advance payment of $150 or more. You can do the job better yourself or contact RAM Research for a list of secured cards.

Finally, don't forget what I learned years ago: no matter how much money you make, when you go out in the world it's better to pay your own way each month than to ride on someone else's train.

STEP 4

Stick Your Head in the Sand

The stock market has a mind of its own.

I don't need radar to find the kitchen when my wife is baking cookies. Just a whiff from the oven is enough. My favorite is almond twist. If you have ever tasted almond twists with orange juice, your mouth is more than likely watering right about now. I'm always told to keep my hands off the cookies until they cool. When they are still hot, you have to shift the cookie from hand to hand. They are what I call "two-handed" cookies. Anyone can eat cold, one-handed cookies, but the temptation to eat two-handed cookies is too great for me to resist.

Which leads me to the widely held belief that you have to actively manage your investments to make money. The truth is that those who invest and do nothing are often the big winners. Like keeping your hands off the cookies until they are cool, keeping your hands off your investments is one of the most difficult things for investors to do.

Your heart is suddenly pounding as you think about the hair-raising dive in the stock market and how much money you are losing. All you can think about is how to get out of the stock market and save what is left of your nest egg. So you get out and a few days later find yourself holding the proceeds—which you have to pay capital gains taxes on—as the stocks you just sold soar back to new highs. Worse yet, if you want to get back in, you'll have to buy back high-priced stocks with what cash you have left.

This lesson is so important that I'm going to tell you again why so many people lose money in the stock market: *They can't sit on their hands and leave their investments alone.* Warren E. Buffett and I were both born and raised in Omaha, Nebraska. We both love trains, although he loves Cherry Coke and I hate soft drinks, but we both invest the same way: Once invested, we tend to stand pat and stay in the market. While I might not always have been able to sleep soundly over the years when the stock market took a roller coaster ride with my money invested, the huge gains I've made could only have occurred by following Buffett's lead and keeping my hands off my money.

When I was growing up my parents packed me off to my aunt's farm each summer across the river in Iowa. One of this city kid's jobs was to help with the milking. Let's just say I wasn't a natural. When I got to Wall Street I realized that the brokers and the stock fund managers, who virtually read their tea leaves to forecast the market and divine the time when stocks were going to rise and fall, did about as well with their predictions as this city kid did with those cows in the barn.

Today, financial soothsaying is a great cottage industry. Newspapers, magazines, and television continually dance riches in front of our eyes and sometimes we feel like fools if we don't grab at the latest opportunity to get rich. Every month in the personal finance magazines, you're enticed by the promise of a hot new mutual fund or stock that's too good to pass up. But the more you read the more you realize that most of the past picks have gone into the

Dumpster. Some have fizzled almost before the ink was dry on the pages.

Recently, I saw a television commercial for a major stockbroker. The bulls were running up Wall Street in panic, yet the announcer asserted that with this firm's help, you could not only avoid being trampled by the herd, but also know which bull to ride to riches. There's only one problem with this ad. The herd on Wall Street carries briefcases and they panic as often as the cattle. This leads me to another important lesson for building wealth:

Wall Street is a giant casino, a game of chance. Anyone who claims to know how to predict the direction of the stock market or an individual stock is simply blowing smoke in your face.

The securities markets in the United States are open, free, and competitive arenas in which large numbers of investors believe that a stock will rise or fall at the same time. The seller thinks it's time to take a profit, the buyer thinks hefty profits lie ahead. The idea, of course, is to determine who is right. In a perfectly efficient market, prices reflect what is known. In the actual stock market, however, prices often reflect the judgment of investors about future events and how these events, if they occur, will affect the market.

In spite of the oldest axiom on Wall Street, that *the market has a mind of its own,* many investors continue to try to outguess the future direction of the market. Here are the most popular market-timing theories.

Random Walk Theory

This theory believes that changes in stock prices will follow what is known on Wall Street as a *random walk.* The random walk theory states that past prices are not a basis for forecasting future prices but, rather, that stock prices reflect reactions to information in a random fashion. Thus, future prices are no more predictable than a haphazard roll of the dice.

One of the best books on investing is Burton G. Malkiel's classic *A Random Walk Down Wall Street* (17th ed., Norton, 2000). Malkiel, a professor at Princeton University and a governor on the American Stock Exchange, watched the market day after day. It dawned on him that investing is really a simple process. A random walk, he said, is one in which you can't predict future actions on past results. Malkiel believes that all the chart readers and investment gurus who try to predict the future of the stock market based on past experiences are wasting their time.

His book offers the following conclusion: "On Wall Street, the term *random walk* is an obscenity. It is an epithet coined by the academic world and hurled insultingly at the professional soothsayers. But taken to its logical extreme, it means that a blindfolded monkey throwing darts at a newspaper's financial pages could select a portfolio that would do just as well as one carefully selected by the experts."

I think of Malkiel every time I read *The Wall Street Journal*'s regular six-month investment dartboard contest in which the paper pits the performance of four investment professionals against stocks chosen by *Wall Street Journal* staffers tossing darts at the *Journal*'s stock tables on the wall. As if they have leaped from the pages of Malkiel's book, the agents of chance regularly wallop the pros.

Technical Theory

Those who follow a technical analysis approach challenge the random walk theory. Technicians follow the graphs of stock prices, the advance-decline line, the cumulative total of advancing stocks minus declining stocks, and trading volume. Their charts of past performance forecast whether a stock will go up or down. The classic *pennant* formation tells us nothing about the market's direction, but it's supposed to tell us if a breakout will occur soon. In addition, whenever it does, whether the direction is up or down, the tech followers say it should continue in that direction for a while. Devotees of this method of looking at the past confidently feel they can predict the future of individual stocks and the stock market. They're right about half the time.

Fundamental Theory

Those who follow the fundamental analysis approach work outside the market. They try to forecast stock prices by analyzing a company's market share, balance sheet, products, management, and the expected demand for its products or services. By using this method, fundamentalists believe they can tell when a stock or group of stocks is undervalued or overvalued at the current market price.

Based on these theories regarding the price movements of stocks, there is a never-ending supply of books and kits on how to make money in stocks. They purport to give you the inside story on the techniques used by professional traders. The authors say they know how to identify the numbers in a company balance sheet that every investor should be concerned about, how to read economic indicators that flash warning signals of market changes well in advance, and how market action in major stock groups foretells market turning points.

Here's the bottom line: No matter which system you use, unforeseen events can change a stock price overnight and even the pros can frequently lose their shirts. It may seem reasonable to believe that investors, using the latest market forecasting methods, should be able to achieve a better-than-average return. However, from my years of experience, I have concluded that both chartists and fundamentalists are clouding the real issue: *The stock market has a mind of its own.*

I want to repeat this just in case you missed it before. Trying to outguess the direction of the stock market by buying and selling stocks at just the right time gets no better results on average than having an orangutan throw darts at newspaper stock tables stuck on the wall. Market timing is an illusion. No one can know when stock prices will rise or fall. No one. Not brokers, financial planners, mutual fund managers, newsletter writers, or anyone else can consistently buy low and sell high. Although market timers may reduce short-term risks by exiting the market when it declines, they can lose huge returns when they are not fully invested when the market rallies. In real life, today's hottest stock can come crashing down tomorrow when Alan Greenspan brings the market to its knees.

Experts' Scorecard

Investment Newsletters

Mark Hulbert, who writes *The Hulbert Financial Digest,* a newsletter that tracks the results of investment newsletters, says, "The primary virtue of market-timing newsletters isn't beating the market. In fact, their virtue lies in their ability to reduce risk by more than return, which is forfeited in the process. This is not a realistic goal, however, because market timers also are trying to reduce risk." One way to reduce risk is to invest only half in stocks and hold the balance in cash, but Hulbert cautions that with this strategy your rate of return would also be about half as much as the stock market's.

Hulbert says over the past twenty- and fifteen-year periods only a few newsletters (Hulbert rates the performance of sample portfolios created by more than 150 financial newsletters) beat the total return for his benchmark gauge, the Wilshire 5000 index total return. (For more information check the website at www.cbsmarket watch.com or write *The Hulbert Financial Digest,* 5051-B Backlick Road, Alexandria, VA 22003; or call 703-750-9060.)

James Schmidt, editor of *The Timer Digest,* a newsletter that tracks the performance of market-timing newsletters, compares their performance to that of the S&P 500 stock index, which is set at 100.00 at the start of any given comparison. The S&P 500 index is a broad-based measurement of the changes in stock market prices based on the average performance of 500 widely held large-cap common stocks. For the one-year period from July 14, 1999, to July 1, 2000, only the top ten market-timers beat the S&P 500 index, but when the market made a major correction, from April 14, 2000, to July 14, 2000, only four of the top ten market-timing newsletter writers beat the S&P 500 stock index. (For more information check the website at www.timerdigest.com or write *The Timer Digest,* Box 1688, Greenwich, CT 06836; or call 203-629-3503.)

The so-called *market experts* who write investment newsletters try every imaginable device to become the long-term Timer of the Year. One of the winners was Arch Crawford, who writes *The Crawford Perspectives.* His secret of knowing when to buy and sell stocks? He times the market with astrology. He picks buy-and-sell opportunities by using a combination of planetary cycles with the moon and stars. In a recent issue, Crawford tells his readers, "We forecast an extreme solar event, and skies will light up with massive harmonic planetary aspects. The next day, a new moon at perigee (closest passage to the Earth) creates the exact worst combination. Watch for abnormalities in weather, earthquakes, and financial markets." Crawford warns that the position of Mars can also portend tight money and a currency crisis.

On August 1, 2000, Crawford told his readers, "We believe the solar eclipse on July 30 timed the short-term low for now. A strong advance from current levels should create a gain of +30 to +100 S&P 500 index points or +240 to 800 Dow Jones Industrial Average points over the next 10 days." Ten days later, the S&P 500 index was near a record 1,500, and the Dow Industrials had gone over the 11,000 mark for the first time since the previous April.

In his story in *Forbes* magazine (September 11, 1995), Hulbert writes: "I'm not festooning my office wall with astrological charts or staying up late nights with the works of Nostradamus. I'm only saying that results are what counts and, since results are what Arch Crawford has produced, I will take him seriously—whatever I may think about astrology." (For more information, check the website at www.astromoney.com or write *Crawford Perspectives,* 6890 Sunrise Drive #120-70, Tucson, AZ 85750; or call 520-577-1158.)

With investors lacking any other successful method of picking stocks, the age of financial astrology is apparently on the upswing. There is even an astrologer's mutual fund for those who believe sunspots translate into a sell signal on Wall Street.

Many newsletter writers and brokers love to tout the hottest stocks in the market, telling tales of huge profits that await the savvy investor. However, a study by the Babson Group of mutual funds found that the hottest stocks on the market in each of the past eleven years, stocks that many investors fell all over themselves to buy, have performed miserably. More than half of them actually declined in price while the S&P 500 stock index doubled.

The fall of these so-called hot stocks was no accident. The companies were often at the cutting edge of a new technology or a new type of business when their stocks skyrocketed. In every instance, the promise of rapid growth brought many competitors into these companies' markets, soon diminishing their seemingly brilliant prospects.

Despite their sorry track record of predicting the next hot stock and when to buy and sell, the investment newsletter writers never quit. And why should they? At an average cost of some $250 a year, they continue to make money telling eager investors how and when to buy and sell on Wall Street. Are high-priced investment newsletters worthwhile? Mark Hulbert, writing in *Forbes* (June 7, 1993), says that, based on his study, "There is absolutely no correlation between higher price and better performance. If anything, it is just the reverse. Over the past five years, the 20 percent of letters with the lowest subscription fees had the best average performance. These inexpensive newsletters produced a compound annual return of 15.2 percent. In contrast, those letters in the costliest price range returned 10.5 percent." (During this same period, the overall stock market had an annual return of 15.4 percent.)

One monthly newsletter, which between issues provided a telephone hot line with daily updates at an annual cost of $995, was no bargain. If you had followed its advice over the years, you would have failed to earn even the Treasury bill rate. Another investment letter with a subscription cost of $650 a year actually lost 77 percent over a five-year period on its portfolio.

A disturbing trend has developed among some investment newsletters. In an attempt to lower costs, many have turned into little more than hidden advertising messages for financial firms. One major letter says, "Enclosures are paid advertisements. The newsletter is not endorsing any specific company or product. This revenue defrays the cost of producing this newsletter and mailing to you." Another notes that, "As you are aware, inserts carried in this newsletter are paid for by fee and commission. This helps to keep our subscription rates down while enabling us to maintain the quality of services to our subscribers." When you are paying big bucks for help on where to invest, I don't believe you should have to wade through paid commercials to learn what the writer has to say, and then wonder how objective he or she is.

Pension Fund Managers

If investment newsletters can't outguess the stock market, what about pension fund managers working with billions of dollars? In its October 25, 1993, issue entitled "Money Business," *Forbes* found that American business spends $9 billion a year on money managers for their employee pension plans, and most of the spending is futile. "One study from the Brookings Institution shows that the average professional investment manager lagged behind the unmanaged S&P 500 stock index by 2.6 percent per year over seven years. A good part of this lag," *Forbes* says, "can be traced not to stupidity or incompetence, but to the simple fact that trading stocks and supervising money managers costs money." The question *Forbes* asks is, "Why shouldn't the average American company just fire its squadrons of money managers and put its pension money into an index fund with low turnover and minimal fees?" As one expert put it: "It's like monkeys trading bananas in trees. The money managers end up with a lot of bananas."

Stockbrokers

Can you trust your broker to tell you when and what to buy? Like everyone else in the business of predicting stock prices, brokers are right about as often as the roll of the dice. In the past few years, however, the broker's analysts have issued glowing buy or strong buy recommendations on the same stocks the firm was underwriting. Often these buy recommendations followed the stock down from $80 to $15 a share. Consider this recommendation of one stock analyst: "We believe that the recent weakness in the price of most stocks presents a buying opportunity rather than an excuse to raise cash. In our opinion, the underlying fundamentals have not changed sufficiently to warrant a more cautious attitude toward equities. With the price of most stocks down by varying degrees, it is timely to seek out those with relatively solid fundamentals that have been caught in the market's downdraft, along with issues with relatively less attractive prospects."

You have to be one savvy investor on Wall Street to figure out this message. Or consider this brokerage recommendation: "Currently trading at 29 times our fiscal 2001 earnings per share estimate of $1.53, we believe the shares are undervalued. Earnings per share warrant a 12-month target price of $48." Six months later the shares had tumbled 50 percent, trading near a 52-week low of $21.

When Wall Street yells "strong buy," watch your wallet. During the market crash of 2000–2001 most broker analysts continued to issue buy signals on stocks that continued to fall in price. As a result, many investors have little respect for ratings from in-house stock analysts at brokerages or, as they are known on the Street, *sell-side analysts,* because they work for the people selling stock. During this period well over 90 percent of the analysts give a stock a strong buy or a moderate buy recommendation. That basis to buy is built into their job because retail brokers need recommended stocks to sell to their clients and sales commissions are a big part of their income. If they are uncertain about a stock, you may find in-house stock analysts issuing a long-term accumulate recommendation. Seldom, however, do you find a hold rating for a stock. It simply is bad for business. When a brokerage firm downgrades a stock to hold, that's a subtle way of saying sell, and this signal can often be translated into the fact that you should have been out of the stock a few weeks ago.

You will also be a savvy investor if you avoid acting on most of what is said about the market and the insider tips on Wall Street by the head and shoulder talkers on the financial cable network shows. I'm the host of a nationwide live call-in radio program and have been a guest on numerous financial cable shows, so I can say with authority that the media has an insatiable need for talking heads—many of whom attract attention precisely for their contrarian positions. Just because you see them dispensing advice on television doesn't mean it applies to you.

The Basics Work

The good news is that the basics of investing continue to work and they are simple to understand. You just have to invest in a few good performing blue-chip stocks that have consistently made money and then, like an ostrich, stick your head in the sand and ignore the latest insider tips. The bad news and flameouts on Wall Street can't hurt you. What can hurt you is your panic forcing you to do something about the news. If you learn to stay in the stock market at all times, through market crashes and record Dows, what you paid for this book will be returned to you many times over.

For example, consider an investor's panic attacks, heart palpitations, and frayed nerves as he watched the stock market continue to tumble the first few months of 2001. Frustrated investors asked, "Stay in the market with these plunging numbers? The Dow Industrials are only about 9,300." This could make anyone sick. Then, in the month of April, the Dow Jones Industrial Average was up a hefty 8.7 percent, or a gain of 856 points. This wiped out all the previous year's losses and pushed the average ahead of its close at the end of April the previous year. Then by mid-May 2001 the Dow Industrials had soared to 11,300—only about 400 points below the all-time record high.

Here's another example of the value of staying put. In the summer of 1929, a young man, at his father's suggestion, put the $400 he had earned on odd jobs into a mutual fund. Almost before the ink was dry on his investment receipt, the biggest stock market crash in history shattered Wall Street. By 1933, the value of his investment had fallen to just $85. With this kind of loss, he decided to stay in the market, but he never put any more money in what appeared to him a losing proposition. Today, his original $400 investment is worth more than $40,000.

On a more recent note, those who invested in General Electric stock in 1981, when the price was about $1.10 a share, made huge gains in the next twenty years with a stock price around $47.00 at the end of the period. During this period, GE recorded twenty years of consecutive quarterly earnings increases. No one knows in advance when to be in or out of the market, but the rewards for the courageous that stay in can be breathtaking. Why?

More than 95 percent of the gain in the stock market in an average year can occur in just a few trading days.

Here's how your annual return could have been affected if you were not invested at all times during a typical five-year period.

THE BULL MARKET FROM 1983 TO 1987

Time in the Stock Market	Average Annual Total Return with Dividends (percent)
Invested for all 1,276 trading days	26.3
Out of the market the best 20 days	13.1
Out of the market the best 40 days	4.3

The numbers don't lie. If you were out of the market for only the forty best trading days during this five-year period, your average annual return fizzled to just 4.3 percent, nearly the same as a money market return. With these kinds of results, I'm amazed that most people have such a hard time holding on to their investments. For the most part, the sellers are sitting on the sidelines like Nero watching Rome burn. Locked out of a stock market that's on fire with record growth, they are stuck in an investor's nightmare.

I've talked on the air with Bill Berger, president of the Berger Funds of Denver, Colorado, about his long career in building shareholders' wealth. Bill knows the value of staying in the market at all times. He says, "You can liken the situation to a man walking his dog. He's going from point A to point B by following a path of growing earnings. His dog, much like the stock market, is running off in different directions, chasing a rabbit, and barking at a squirrel. The man is too wise to wear himself out following the dog; he knows the dog, and the stock market, will be with him at point B when he gets there."

Most people who read this book might think I'm kidding them. It can't be that simple for a novice to make a lot of money. But it is. Just consider that *Money* magazine, in the August 1995 issue, told its readers, "The new way to make money in funds today is to start with index funds and add the market beaters." *Money* said that few stock funds outperform the market and low-cost, market-tracking index funds do best. Or consider this quote from the June 1996 issue of *Smart Money* magazine: "You can't beat the market—so why even try? The only sensible thing to do is put all your money in an index fund, such as a Standard & Poor's 500 stock index fund, and take whatever the market gives you."

The good news for those who stay in the market at all times with an index or good stocks is that the Dow Jones Industrial Average has continued to rise over the years. Sometimes we forget just how fast the Dow (and the stock market) has been soaring. Stick with me as we look at the Dow Industrial index.

The Dow, named after Charles Dow, was created in 1884 as a way to gauge the daily direction of the stock market. The average contained twelve stocks and opened at 40.94. In 1928, the Dow was expanded to include 30 stocks (the current number), and the stocks included in the index have been updated twenty times since then.

From 1884 to 1984 the Dow Industrials were less than 1,000. Despite the worst market sell-off since the Great Depression, when the Dow tumbled more than 500 points in 1987, it took only another four years for the Dow to close above 3,000. Then the Dow shifted into high gear with the bull market of the 90s. By 1995, the Dow had climbed above 8,000. Five years later, at the end of the century, the Dow Industrials had broken though the 11,000 level. If this same rate of growth continues for another ten years, the Dow Industrial Average could be around 30,000!

What risk do you run by staying in the market at all times? If you stay in the stock market for only one year, you can run a significant risk. The performance of common stocks between 1926 and 1992 varied from a best annual return of 54 percent to a worst loss of 43 percent. However, through periods of high inflation, market crashes, and wars, one important point is clear: The longer you hold stocks, the less chance you run of losing money. Over a ten-year period, for example, the risk of owning stocks has been almost zero. Over time, investors have borne the full brunt of the 1929 stock market crash and the subsequent Great Depression, and they went through the prolonged bear market of the mid-1970s, when stocks as a whole lost 40 percent in two years. The worst ten years for investors was 1928 to 1937, during which time they had about a 23 percent total return. Throughout the postwar years, investors who put their heads in the sand and invested made money. The average ten-year return since 1924 has been 10.9 percent: $1,000 invested then would be worth $4 million now.

Or, to further illustrate why it's important to stay in the market for a few years, consider the Standard & Poor's 500 stock index.

The major moves included a crushing 26.5 percent loss in 1977. In 1978 it was up 6.6 percent, then down 4.9 percent in 1981, then up a hefty 21.4 percent in 1982, then down 3.2 percent in 1990, then up 30.5 percent in 1991, then down 9.1 percent in 2000. Again, to earn the best return over this period, it was important not only to stay in the market at all times, but to continue to invest regularly. The good news is that when the bear markets of 1973–74, 1981–82, and 1990–91 finally ended, the blue-chip Standard & Poor's 500 index was up 25, 37, and 25 percent respectively just four months later.

If the past is any indicator, to match the stock market returns in the future, you don't need good-luck charms and the assurance of a fortune teller, you just need common sense to invest in a few blue-chip stocks with increasing earnings and stay invested at all times, ride out the down years and profit from the double-digit years, and have the guts to avoid the temptation of the latest "hot" investment tip.

On the other hand, avoiding an investment in the stock market because of the chance of a loss is a little like avoiding a train ride because of a possible wreck. Life is full of uncertainties, but investing long-term in the stock market is among the least of them.

I wish I could say that acquiring wealth is difficult, but it isn't. I learned that much from the farmers. But for someone who has been trapped in the lifelong process of bill paying, it takes courage to save and invest regularly despite one's fears of the stock market. I hope you have the courage to let the market make you money as it has for a farm kid who loves to play with trains. I know it can.

STEP 5

Invest with Technology

If you've lost your way in today's fast-moving electronic investment services and you can't see the forest for the trees, the chances are you've already lost money.

When the only investment model was a personal stockbroker, a life insurance agent, or a bank, the number of places to put your money was limited by two things: the products offered by the firms, and the span of awareness that one broker or banker could have.

Financial deregulation, however, has allowed banks, brokers, and financial planners to invade each other's turf for the first time and offer one-stop shopping. This flood of information has overwhelmed most people, and for many has become downright confusing. You can now invest in mutual funds, FDIC-insured savings accounts, and annuities; buy life insurance; or buy or sell stock from almost any financial firm or sales representative. The vast array of investments and savings products developed out of a self-feeding cycle. Independent investors wanted different or better performing funds, the Internet and personal finance magazines provided performance numbers and new investment opportunities, and financial companies could now reach millions of investors in America with a click of a button. As a result, more than 8,000 mutual funds and other new investments sprang up and, not surprisingly, each was billed as the right investment for you.

The biggest change in the way we invest, however, occurred in the 1990s with the combination of the Internet and the online discount broker. In fact, most investors today use online discount stockbrokers to trade stocks and buy and sell mutual funds. And the growth of online trading has only begun: 3.8 million new online trading accounts were opened in the last six months of 2000, an 87 percent increase compared to one year earlier. And now there are an estimated 10 million people trading stocks online. At least twenty-six discount brokers offer selected mutual funds with no transaction fees so you can buy or sell from different fund families through one broker and save time and paperwork.

The telephone expanded the options to invest without a visit to your local broker, but the Internet opened up the entire broker's office to worldwide investing. If you have a computer that is connected to the Internet, you can explore the world of managing and changing your investments online. Let's look at how anyone can start investing online.

Online Trading

You've probably seen ads for easy to use web-access computers and i-terminals like Earthlink (www.mailstation.com). These and other low power email and browser personal computers are commonly called *Internet appliances* or *Web Enabled Terminals.* While these systems appear to offer an excellent value and easy access to the Internet for trading or email, they have pitfalls. The majority of these products are too under-powered to perform stock trading and their primary purpose appears to be to lock you into a long-term service contract for an Internet connection. Avoid those tempting cash rebates of $75 to $400 that require activation of a contract for 36 months of Internet service. The chances are that over the next three years new, cheaper, and faster Internet connections will be available, and you'd be stuck with a long-term contract. These cash rebate offers are the computing version of cell phone plans. It's important to understand the fine print and your commitments and exit expenses before you agree to the contract.

Because the typical Internet appliance is so restrictive in performing many tasks, you should purchase a medium-powered desktop personal computer and monitor. These generally cost under $700 complete. You can then select your own Internet service and have a powerful enough computer to not only trade stocks, mutual funds, and bonds on the Internet but also run most finance programs, word processing, and even the occasional computer game for the kids. As for which companies you pick for your Internet provider, remember the most costly service is not always the best. Everything is a tradeoff. Standard phone line service from Earthlink, MSN, Mindspring, and other providers are usually less than $35 a month. Low-rate service is available from AOL or AT&T for $5 to $10 a month if you limit your hours. If you want faster speed for your surfing, consider a cable modem, MCI wireless dish, or DSL service. Any of these can cost between $30 and $70 per month, depending on where you live. Speed is not the only advantage; these services are always on if your computer is on, and there is no interference with phone calls on your regular line. Another option is to use Internet access terminals at cafés, airports, libraries, or hotels. Many are free for ten minutes, and those that charge are usually reasonable.

Online Trading Benefits and Options

Any electronic trading account you establish will be accessed through the Internet, the global backbone of information transfers. This allows you to access your account worldwide through your personal computer, at a friend's house, or through any public terminal. I have had great success checking our investments from a café in Paris and a small kiosk in Tokyo. With the new mobile web services available on personal managers such as the Palm Wireless, the RIM BlackBerry, or Web Ready Phones (called WAP) like the Handspring Treo, you can monitor your investments anytime, anywhere. Sometimes investment houses such as Fidelity or E*Trade will even give you these devices for free if you maintain a large balance and perform regular transactions.

With an online trading account you can buy stocks, bonds, mutual funds, futures, metals, and even options such as pork bellies, gold, and yen. But the major benefit of performing your trades electronically is the cost. Trades performed electronically require so little provider intervention that the normal cost of $50 for a large trade today is $200 less than the cost of the same trade in the early 1980s. Cost for small trades can range from $50 to near $5!

There are over 7,000 SIPC-registered brokerages, only eight to ten of which declare bankruptcy each year. To give you some piece of mind, your broker should have Securities Investor Protection Corp (SIPC) insurance to cover cash and securities (similar to FDIC insurance, which banks have to cover deposits) to compensate their customers when the brokerage goes bankrupt. The insurance does not, however, protect investors from a bad investment, or a dishonest broker who pockets the cash and heads south. Therefore, it's a good idea to contact the National Association of Securities Dealers (NASD) (800-289-9999; www.nasd.com) to determine whether the broker or the brokerage firm has a history of disciplinary actions or criminal or civil actions.

Setting Up an Account

To set up an online brokerage account you need to allow at least a week. Even in this age of simultaneous market trades and fast e-commerce, the act of setting up a new account is a slow and traditional process. Part of this time is used by the Securities and Exchange Commission to make sure that you are actually a qualified investor and able to responsibly handle your own market purchase and sell decisions. Be prepared to answer a standard list of questions about your trading experience and years you have been active in managing your investments. Online brokerage firms ask these specific questions to protect themselves in the event you have a dispute with them. Don't be afraid to tell the truth if you have little or no experience in trading stocks and bonds. Many firms such as E*Trade may ask you to read an educational mailing before they open your account. Several of the very low fee brokerage firms actually require you to complete a multi-page test to qualify for an account. They want to make sure new customers are savvy enough to trade securities on their own and keep their costs low with fewer customer support services.

Funds can be sent in to your brokerage account by check or wire, but even with wired funds, expect a wait of at least three days for the money to be credited to your account. If the bank that holds your money market account has their own online broker, then you can tap the funds already in your account. With cash readily available, it is possible to do same day buys with account openings, but expect them to limit your purchase to $10,000, no matter how much money you have in your account.

In researching electronic brokers, consider what level of support you will need to make your trades. Online discount brokerage firms normally allow some but usually not all of the following:

- Internet-activated online electronic trades
- Telephone command keys or voice recognition to make trades
- Telephone trades
- A local broker's office to trade

The minimum transaction fees for trades placed on the Internet can run from as low as $5 to $75 or higher. Trades over the phone or during a visit to the broker's office carry a higher cost. Most brokers have maximum transaction fees and different break points in steps depending on the size of the trade.

The actual execution of your buy or sell orders can occur much later at a higher or lower price than the price at the time you placed the order.

Smell something burning? You may discover it's your stock portfolio crashing. You race to your discount broker for the latest information. Then you discover that most of the information on the web is *at least* 20 minutes old, delayed so that real-time quote services can charge a premium for their services.

But it is possible to get free real-time quotes of the market from your online broker if you go through an additional step of reading a dozen or so pages of legal disclosure terms on how not to use the data you will be viewing. If your broker does not have this option, or you do not have a brokerage account, several smaller stock information sites will allow you access to their market feed by registering with them, usually for free. Dedicated direct ticker systems are available for about $39 a month or more and can be set up in any home or office with a high-speed Internet connection.

With heavy volume, or with so-called hot stocks, the trades can stack up and usually the best customers get the priority for execution. These include the big mutual funds and major clients of the brokers. For instant real-time execution of trades you need a multi-monitor, multi-market, mega trading computer system. This is called a level 2 trading system and requires a direct market connection at a cost of around $250 a month. These are similar to the stock display systems you've seen Wall Street traders use on television, and they are for serious day traders who need instant order execution. Ask your current or prospective online broker for his average transaction time chart. They are also available at many sites on the Internet that compare brokers and they look similar to the airlines' on-time charts.

Examples of firms with the basic levels of services are: Brown & Co, Datek, TD Waterhouse, Ameritrade, E*Trade. Firms with higher fees and service include: Wells Fargo Brokerage, Merrill Lynch, and Salomon Smith Barney.

Single Click Investing

You're now online with a discount broker and you want to invest in some stocks, so you hit the Send button on your personal computer. The lights blink and your order is on its way directly to the corner of Broad and Wall streets in New York.

To see what happens next, let's follow an order placed through an online broker. We'll use a discount broker with a fictional name of All-Trade, or AT for short. After your computer dials into the Internet through your ISP, you log onto AT's web site. Next, you sign in and provide your password. Once that is recognized, your computer will lock into the server at AT using encrypted data to provide financial security. A lock icon on the lower bar of your browser software usually indicates this. Once you enter your online discount brokerage account, your screen should display the current cost and volume of the stock you are interested in buying.

Say you decide to buy 100 shares of MSFT (Microsoft) because it is falling in price and you believe the stock will rebound to a higher price. You enter the information on the "Market Order" screen and hit the send button. *Never hit the send button more than once!* What happens if you get impatient and hit the send button again? Chances are the first order was placed even though the computer did not respond that it was completed. With the second click of the send button, you could own twice as much stock as you wanted. In the best case, you have a margin account, or the second order was refused due to insufficient funds.

Next, your order is entered into the buy queue at AT. If the market order desk is busy, or your chosen stock order desk is busy, the discount broker's queue could be quite long. A second server at AT checks the buy and sell orders and passes them on to the server at their brokerage portal on Wall Street. Most discount or online firms do not actually have a *seat* on the exchange; they buy access to the computer system of a major brokerage house and process their orders through them. This usually works well when there is extra capacity on the brokerage server to handle AT's business. Unfortunately, if your stock or fund has been shooting out the lights and now is plunging down the charts, the rush of sell orders from AT customers could receive second priority behind the brokerage house's institutional buyers, mutual funds, and their regular customers.

At that point the processing of the queue at AT slows down. An order may not reach the market floor for execution for several hours or even before the market closes for very different prices that you wanted. If the delay in order execution costs you money, your broker may waive the transaction fee for selling your stock after it plunged an additional 20 percent before the discount broker could execute the trade! For this reason, many investors keep two online trading accounts, one account with low-cost $9.95 trades for when times are good for casual investing, and another account with an expensive, old-line Wall Street firm to make sure their orders are executed in a timely manner when the market has heavy volume.

Stop Sell Orders

In a stock market that can slash the share price of a stock by as much as 40 percent in a day, most investors fail to take advantage of one of the most important profit protection opportunities: a *stop sell order.* Stop sell orders work like this: If you own a stock that is currently trading for $80 a share and you want to protect yourself in the event of a major sell-off, you might enter a stop sell order at $74 a share. You want the sell price low enough to get you out with the least damage, yet not too tight so the stock will fall below your stop sell price, trigger your sell order, and then rebound to a much higher level. When the stock drops to or below $74 a share, a market order to sell your stock will be generated by the computer and sent to the broker's sell queue. The main advantage is that the automatic sell order can occur before most of the investors in the stock begin to panic and enter their sell orders.

Wireless Trading

As we enter this decade, trading anywhere and anytime has become a reality. This capability will become the way the majority of investors check the market and trade their portfolios. Currently a half dozen online trading firms offer wireless market services on handheld PDA-type devices, Internet-enabled cell phones, and two-way pagers. Stock information and trading is performed on a small device with a screen large enough to track your stock and place buy or sell orders. Most of these devices require you to subscribe to a special wireless service plan that generally runs between $10 and $50 extra per month. The transaction fees for any trades are additional. Two-way pagers have a small keyboard that also allows you to send and receive email anywhere, even in a meeting. As of this writing, tracking the market or trading with these devices is slower than doing the same thing on a personal computer. In addition, trading through these devices may add additional delays to the online trading cycle already described. Still, there's no question that the flexibility they offer is amazing. To check on wireless services and verify trading plans and prices, log onto ww.schwab.com, www.fidelity.com, www.etrade.com, www.tdwaterhouse.com, and www.ameritrade.com.

Using the Internet to Manage Your 401(k)

If your employer has a 401(k) plan, check to see if the investment provider offers Internet access to your account. Funds managed by Fidelity, Vanguard, and other large funds all have personal access accounts where you can view your current balances, change distribution of your investments, and access other information about the fund. In addition, some programs offered to corporations allow plan participants to use the firm's brokerage services at a substantial discount.

Finally, when looking on the Internet for help in deciding what online brokers to select, visit Epinions.com and www.cyberinvest.com to see how others rate the brokers you're considering. Also keep an eye out for special annual issues of financial magazines that rank electronic brokerages on a number of criteria, including execution reliability.

Portfolio Tracking and Money Management

The Internet is filled with useful portfolio tracking programs and they are available from most online brokers. Before you select one look for these two attributes:

- **Security or anonymity.** You should find a site that does not require you to divulge personal information to access the tracking program you want to use. You don't want a company to learn the details of your investments and start sending you solicitations for additional investments. In addition, you want a password entry system easy enough to use daily, but hard enough so others can't look at your personal portfolio.

- **Breadth of information.** This is especially important if you happen to invest in a smaller company or less known mutual fund. Sites that are investor favorites are finance.yahoo.com, www.marketwatch.com, and www.thestreet.com.

Accounting programs such as Quicken or Microsoft Money are also good ways to organize and track your investments. Both can help you organize your portfolios of stocks, money market, or mutual funds and give you real-time data with a click of a mouse as long as you have an Internet connection. ASP (Applications Service Provider) software is a popular way of running programs on your computer through a central Internet server. Instead of loading a new program on your PC from a CD-ROM like Quicken, you can run the program off the Internet and it loads your PC each time you log onto your account. There is no need to fill up your hard drive or update your software. Another advantage is remote access—you can monitor your finances from a beachfront hotel in Hawaii if that's where fate finds you. Virtual money management with ASP software is available from such companies as www.net ledger.com, which also provides free trial accounting and money management programs that can be accessed and updated anywhere in the world.

There are also all-in-one reporting sites such as www.myciti.com by Citicorp. This site is a one-stop web page that displays your savings, checking, and investment balances regardless of what bank they are in. It also can show your balances for the phone, power, and gas bills.

Online Banking and Insured Investing

For banks that began as brick-and-mortar institutions, online banking is simply a more convenient way to interact with the same customers they've always done business with. On the other hand, purely online banks such as E-trade or Wingspan have no physical bank location. They operate out of regular office buildings and have third-party companies handle the check entry and printing functions. They are fully licensed banks in the states where they offer services and may provide Federal Deposit Insurance on your savings. These online banks attract savings accounts by offering higher interest rates than traditional banks; they avoid the brick-and-mortar costs of a local bank and pass some of those savings along in the form of higher returns on deposits. Online banks are usually tied to an online brokerage service and thus offer a new level of money management that would not be possible at the local brick-and-mortar bank. They can hold your checking account money in an easy-to-access money market account, which allows you to move your money into stocks, bonds, or mutual funds. In the traditional bank, the funds would have to be wired to the brokerage house to buy the stock, or you would have to physically deliver a check. With your money all in one place you can move it about to maximize your gains, and more important, easily create a diversified portfolio of high- and low-risk investments.

The downside is moving money in and out of the electronic bank. The local bank has a branch office with a teller and an ATM. The electronic bank may also have an ATM in that it allows you to use one of the systems of national ATMs. But without a walkup teller, your other option is to write a check, cash it at local bank, or wire the money to the broker.

Electronic Bill-Paying Services

Revolutions in electronic banking have now made the scary act of electronic funds transfers appear easy and painless. With its friendly new name, electronic bill paying, these transfers will some day be a common part of our personal financial activity. For some, it's already a way of life. The service makes routine payments and dispatches them to your mortgage or power company at the last possible minute to maximize the interest you are earning in your money market checking account. These services are already available for free from some banks and Internet sites, but most charge fees. The main benefits are the maximization of your interest and minimization of late payment charges.

The bad news is that you've already heard the good news. The major problem is that the EBP service you are using must have a direct wire relationship with the companies you want to pay for the service to deliver on its potential advantages. If they can't pay your gasoline bill directly to Shell, for example, they will actually cut a check and send it through the U.S. mails. While many companies are in the EBP system, many are not, and the check/mail system can cost you late payment fees and interest—that is, they may schedule the printing and mailing of your check too late to make it to the creditor by its stated due date. If you read the fine print of the company's agreement, you'll see that they aren't generally responsible for late fees due to their errors or the late arrival of your payment.

In the future, these bill-paying systems will actually scan the requests for payment (formerly called bills), check them for out-of-the-ordinary charges, and schedule them for payment. When the system encounters problems or suspects billing errors or overruns, the EBP system will email you a note about the problem. Major companies that offer electronic bill paying are www.gefn.com, www.statusfactory.com, and www.paymybills.com.

Finding Quality Investment Information

The web has many places to find the information you need to make decisions about investment choices. Most of them are free. Those that charge fees are generally worth it! One of the best free sites is www.financialsavvy.com, where you can click www.bigcharts.com and get a potential investment's one, five, ten or more years' performance at a glance. www.marketwatch.com will let you load your portfolio and, without charge, allows you to check on your holdings at any time. finance.yahoo.com is catching up with its chart overlay feature, which allows easy comparison of any two or more stocks to each other. Subscription services such as www.thestreet.com can provide valuable information as well. The government provides SEC reports at www.sec.gov, and both www.nasdaq.com and www.nyse.com have valuable information.

The Risk of Technology Investing

With the help of the computer, new ways to invest have evolved. While they offer undisputed access and flexibility, you still need to use common sense to get the best results. Just like the trends in retail, the point of electronic services has been to drop the middleman and go direct to the customer. While this approach works well for toys or books where the products are easily understood, it may not work as well when the products include investments and money management. Unless you have the experience or knowledge to combine old-fashioned money management with the speed of an online computer, you can find yourself in financial trouble in the blink of an eye.

The number one pitfall to avoid when you use the new technology to invest your money is taking actions that get you in over your head. Near-unlimited access to your investments means you must be that much more vigilant in fighting the temptation to change investments quickly (and perhaps rashly). Just because you can execute trades with the click of the mouse hundreds of times a day doesn't mean you should!

STEP 6

Build Your Own Portfolio

The more they buy,
The more you make

The heady, get-rich-quick mentality of the 90s has faded in the ashes of the dot-com crash and the technology bust. In its place today is the realization that old-fashion values that made people rich in the past will work again.

I learned these values many years ago when I started on Wall Street. One day a trader on the floor of the New York Stock Exchange grabbed my arm, walked me over to the horseshoe-shaped rooms just off the floor, and gave me some advice that I have lived by over the years.

"Invest in the favorites, my son," he said. "The best blue chips consistently make money no matter what happens to the overall stock market. In fact, the more people who buy a stock the more likely you are to make a profit."

"Is that all I need to know?" I asked in wonderment.

"Yes," he said. "You can forget about the brokers, financial planners, and the high-priced investment newsletters. They try to predict the direction of a stock or the market, and it can't be done."

For over thirty years, this advice has never failed me. Even in the raging bull market of the nineties, where technology was king, I have avoided the crashing of the dot-coms, Enrons, and Global Crossings. I sleep at night with the comfort of knowing that my favorite stocks will be there in the morning and probably headed for higher prices.

Before you invest, the first thing you need to ask yourself: *Will investors always want to buy the stock?* If you think they will despite a falling markets and raging bull markets, you probably have a stock you can live with for years to come. That's because the price of any stock is based on the number of buy or sell orders at any given time. If enough investors want to keep the stock in their portfolios and sit on their hands during a downturn, the price of the stock won't plunge. If enough investors want to add the stock to their portfolio during market upturns, the price of the stock will rise.

An easy way to find the favorites is to grab the *New York Times* Business Section. Each day the favorites are printed as "Stocks held by the largest number of accounts at Merrill Lynch." While not all the favorites are worth your hard-earned money, some of the stocks in my portfolio have come from this list, including Microsoft, Intel, IBM, and GE. The Spring 2002 edition of *Business-Week* magazine ranked the top fifty companies. Johnson & Johnson was number one, Pfizer number three, Merck number forty, and these drug companies are also included in the list.

Another place to find the favorites is among those companies that make up the Dow Jones Industrial Average. There are thirty stocks in the Dow, including favorites such as Coca-Cola, Citigroup, Alcoa, and Exxon Mobil.

Over the years I've talked with some remarkable people on Wall

Street and in the media. Many of them are famous and their advice is featured on television and in financial magazines. They tell other people what to do with their money, yet much of the time they fail to beat the average guy who just invests in the entire stock market and then goes off to play golf.

If you are hungry for some profits and discouraged by the worst back-to-back years on Wall Street in thirty years, I don't suggest you invest in the entire stock market. Embark on a more modest scale of about twelve to fifteen stocks. With that few stocks you need to be choosy and invest only in the bluest of blue chips.

A Favorite Portfolio

Suppose you had picked the following portfolio of favorites from the Dow 30 companies. The average annual returns, according to Dow Jones & Co as of year-end 2001, were:

Stock	**Five years**	**Ten years**
Walmart Stores	39.1%	15.3%
Citigroup	28.9	33.3
IBM	26.9	20.3
General Electric	21.2	22.7
Johnson & Johnson	20.5	17.2
Alcoa	19.3	18.2
Intel	14.1	35.6
Average of the 7 stocks	24.2	23.2
Dow Industrials	11.0	14.6
S&P 500 stock index	10.7	12.9

In this portfolio of favorites, the seven stocks returned, on average, about 24 percent each year for the five years, and 23 percent each year for the ten years.

The long-term performance begins to look even better when you consider the returns of most mutual funds and "undervalued" stocks that made the cover of money magazines the last few years.

If you are shaking your head in disbelief, it's understandable: Over the past five and ten years, these seven favorites, on average, had twice the return of the Dow Jones Industrial Average and the Standard & Poor's 500 stock index. But the stock market is no place to put the grocery money, because investing in equities can be a risky play with any stock subject to sharp and unpredictable swings in its share price.

I should also point out that the favorites don't make money every year. Some years stocks lose money, and in others make money. It's the long-term performance that levels out the soaring and crashing years that counts.

I clearly remember an event that occurred one rainy day just before I left the stock exchange. An experienced trader said, in a way that was sure to get my attention: "Look here, you can make five times in a day what you make in a year in a savings account and you can lose that and more in a single day in the market. But you'll always make more than you lose, and over time that's what will make you rich."

I have also learned that you don't need to be a financial wizard to succeed like Warren Buffett. You just need to understand the basic rules of investing. I wrote this book to share the rules that have shaped my entire career in personal finance. They don't include the latest surefire investment craze, a way to simplify the Elliott Wave theory, or a walk through value or momentum investing, which has taken many investors to the cleaners. Instead, they get right to the heart of making money year in and year out. I believe they are a starting point for anyone looking for a way to build his or her financial future. As a bonus, following these rules could even earn you a little cocktail braggadocio over your earnings.

Jorgensen's Basic Investment Rules

Invest in stocks

A wise man who set performance records on Wall Street once told me, "The risk you take when you put your long-term investments into fixed savings accounts or bonds is that your nest egg won't keep up with inflation while the bulls run wild on Wall Street and stocks leave your savings in the dust."

"So what do you recommend I do?" I asked.

"If you're going to save for more than five years, put most of your money in equities." He went on to explain that over the years stocks made the most money. He was right, it turned out. *USA Today* in April of 2001 reported that nothing beat the performance of equities. Thirty-year Treasury bonds had average annual returns over five years of 1.3 percent; over ten years 0.9 percent; and over twenty years 0.5 percent. That's the good news. The bad news is that investing in hard assets can be as risky as buying Internet or dot-com stocks. Gold over this same period had five-year average annual returns of minus 6.4 percent; ten years, −3.8 percent; and twenty years, −3.5 percent. Collectible gold coins didn't do much better with five-year returns of −0.4 percent; ten-year −2.3 percent; and for twenty years, −2.4 percent. Diamonds may be a girl's best friend, but not for investors. Their five-year average annual return was 1.3 percent; ten years, 1.4 percent; and for twenty years −6.9 percent.

On the other hand, stocks, as measured by the Standard & Poor's 500 stock index during this period had a five-year return of 19.1 percent; ten years, 8.7 percent; and twenty years 11.3 percent. According to the *USA Today* story, only home prices and common stocks have risen faster than the rate of inflation over this period.

Be a standpatter

A *standpatter* is an investor who buys and holds blue-chip stocks for the long term. When Warren Buffett buys a stock, he expects to hold it for at least five years. I like his comment: "Continuing to try to find the best investment is a waste of time. With enough information and a million dollars you can go broke in a year."

A wall poster hangs over my desk. It illustrates why people lose their shirts in the stock market because they can't sit still. It's a picture of a guy in a tight pair of underwear, constantly moving but going nowhere. Why is this important? One of the oldest Wall Street sayings is that *investments that take the least intervention make the most money.* I learned this stuff the hard way; I want you to learn before you get burned.

Mark Hulbert, who writes *The Hulbert Financial Digest,* gives this advice: "After you invest, the most important factor in making money in the stock market is discipline. Discipline to stay in the market turns out to play a far more important role than what many investors think. Without it," Hulbert says, "we are like a sailboat without a rudder, buffeted by every change of direction in which the market's wind blows."

You have to be choosy about your investments, of course, but if you know a company has been in business for twenty years or more, has a bright future, its products are solid, its earnings will continue to grow, and investors will continue to buy the stock, you should hold the stock and continue to invest more.

Reinvest the dividends

Dividends may seem unimportant and it's tempting to spend your stock or mutual fund dividends, but if you use the dividends to automatically buy more shares you'll give your retirement nest egg a big boost in the years to come. *Investor's Business Daily* (August 15, 2000) found that if you had made a one-time investment of $10,000 ten years ago with an 11 percent annual return and you reinvested the dividends you could now have $28,394. If you took your dividends out in cash, you would only end up with $21,000. That's a difference of $7,394, or a 35 percent difference in just ten years. You don't have to be a trader pounding the wooden floors of the New York Stock Exchange or someone who swoops into bargain-hunt out-of-favor stocks to understand that a 35 percent difference over ten years is a *big* number. Like your investments, you simply have to keep your hands off your dividends and let them help you build your retirement nest egg.

Pick the favorites

Once you realize that Wall Street is a big auction house, you can then understand how the price of a stock is determined each day. When a buy or sell order is received on the floor of the exchange it goes to the specialist who is making a market in that stock. They stand ready at any time to buy or sell the stock. The order is typically placed *at market,* which means the trade will take place at whatever price is offered at that time. If several arms are waving sell orders, the specialist could drop the share price. If there is a crowd flashing buy orders, the price of the stock could rise. Remember this valuable tidbit:

At any given time the price of a share of stock is based on the law of supply and demand.

I always invest in stocks that I believe, during a market upturn, will have a long line of buyers in front of the specialist's window. One company might manufacture the insides of an essential product that you'd never see, another might be a household name with a business across America, still another a maker of a drug millions of people need to take each day. I call these stocks my *investment favorites.* To find a favorite stock, look for the following.

Invest in a longtime industry leader

You want a company with a clear lock on its market based on expected continued strong customer demand for its products. Make sure both the company and the industry is in a growing field with solid products and advanced technology.

Invest in a company that has been profitable

The company must have reported strong earnings over a period of at least five years. It has more cash than long-term debt, and its profit margins should be at or above the industry standards. If a company makes a popular product with a well-known brand name, or is a key supplier to an industry, profits will generally follow increased sales.

A company that isn't making money for itself can't make money for you.

Unprofitable companies do occasionally rocket up the charts, but don't bet on them long term. Remember, if your stock is to grow, it needs solid long-term earnings, and when a shakeout occurs, the stocks with good earnings will fare far better in tough markets. Ideally, earnings growth should be accelerating from one quarter to the next, or have increased at around 20 percent a year for the last three years.

Do not invest in retailing, consumer products, or heavy industry

Avoid investing in companies that sell their products through department and grocery stores, or have retail stores. These companies historically have been poor performers. Don't invest in heavy industry like steel, coal, railroads, and lumber. These companies are subjected to wide changes in product demand and from rising imports.

Never invest in a regulated industry

Telephone, electric, gas, or airlines are often limited in what they can charge for their services. If they can't make a lot of money, I don't want to own the stock.

Never invest in companies with a share price below $15

I'm kidding, right? No. If the stock market has a remainder bin, its reserved for under $15 stocks. Value mutual funds have tried to invest in these low-priced out-of-favor stocks and they have lost investors a bundle of money. Wall Street derisively refers to stocks under $10 as "single-digit midgets." At this price level, stocks find it tougher to raise capital by selling shares to the public, employees can lose the value of their stock options, and acquisitions become more expensive as a way to expand. Once the stock falls to less than $5 a share, the chances that the stock will come back over $5 a share is almost zero. At these level stocks tend to fall off Wall Street's radar and are known as *penny stocks.* Let me say this in clear English: When the price of a stock falls below $5 a share, the fat lady has already sung and the party is over.

Make sure the company has a well-known brand name

The reason is that corporate brand familiarity helps attract buyers. A study by Corporate Branding LLC, a brand-strategy consultant, found that for the ten years ended December 31, 1999, a composite of thirty-two companies found to have the strongest brands had a return of 402 percent, compared with 309 percent for the Dow Industrial Average.

Never buy a cheap stock

It's human nature to think a stock you've been following for some time is a bargain after its shares have plunged to new lows. You notice the traffic light has turned from red to amber and you think it's just the right time to step on the gas. But after a stock has taken a big dive, the institutional traders and mutual fund managers have probably already slammed on the brakes and most likely investors in these low-priced stock are headed for a big-time crash.

Make sure the company is at least twenty years old

If you feel compelled to chase the latest hot thing, consider what happened to investors at the start of 2000. Merrill Lynch's Internet Strategies Fund offered to give investors a ride on this red-hot sector and more than one billion dollars poured into the start up fund. The idea was that an Internet fund would be analogous to the biotechnology, health care, and financial funds and offer investors a way to make a broad-based investment in the Internet field.

Thirteen months later, however, the fund had wiped out 71 percent of its value; a $10,000 investment was now worth about $3,000. (Lipper, Inc.; *Wall Street Journal* Market Data Group, May 4, 2001.) A lot of other Internet funds have been liquidated or have changed their name to eliminate any reference to the Internet. From this painful reminder you can learn that when you hitch your star to a new hot stock or sector, it's better to come to the party late, or not at all.

Believe in past performance

Every advertisement you read about the soaring value of a mutual fund or hot stock picks carries this warning: *Past performance is not an indication of future results.* But I've found over the years that you can generally rely on past performance. Not for one year, but if a stock has delivered superior long-term performance over the past three, five, and ten years it will nearly always return much better than average returns the next year. Since we can't see into the future, looking at the past is the best we can do.

Invest in just a few stocks

If you have $10,000 to invest, you could invest in four stocks; with $50,000 maybe seven or eight; and with $100,000, your stock portfolio could include ten to twelve stocks. It's better to invest in just a few stocks you know well than to play the whole market.

Before you invest in any stock (or stock fund), don't rely on a hunch, a tip from a friend, or some head and shoulders on television that has the hot pick of the day. Instead, follow my checklist. It has never failed me. In fact, it saved me from plunging into the Internet craze, avoided the red-hot initial public offering (IPO) market in 2000, and the double-digit losses of 2001.

According to my rules, the winners during the technology and Internet dot-com boom were concentrated in so-called infrastructure companies, companies that actually make a product and dominate their industry, such as networking gear, data storage systems, computer chips, and workstations. The big losers were the companies without a solid product and a long history of increasing profits.

Never Lose Money in the Stock Market!

This is the last and probably the most important of all of my Basic Investment Rules. It should be obvious that no one ever got rich losing money in the stock market, but a lot of investors think they can beat the odds.

Look at the numbers

Your investment account was worth $10,000, and when you talked to your broker or received your mutual fund statement the value was $5,000. You lost 50 percent and the only thing on your mind now is "How do I get even?" But to build your account value back to $10,000 you have to earn a 100 percent return on your money! Let's say you get lucky and earn 9 percent each year for the next eight years. Ignoring taxes, you now have $10,000. But if you were lucky, you have lost again. Had the account remained at $10,000 and you earned the 9 percent each year, your account could now total $20,000.

Take This Quiz

What would you rather do?

a. Invest in a mutual fund with an 80 percent return in one year, and a 50 percent loss the next.
b. Invest in a savings account that paid 5 percent a year.

The answer is consistent growth. At the end of the first year the mutual fund could be worth $18,000. With a 50 percent loss the next, the fund could be worth $9,000. The 5 percent savings account would be worth $11,000 in two years.

A Comparison of Buy-and-Hold and Trend Investing

An investor who invested a dollar sixty years ago and stayed in the stock market at all times could have a portfolio worth about $17,000 today. But if he was out of the market for just the twenty best months in the sixty years, months when the stock market was doing very well, his investment might be worth only $240.

What you are not told as a buy-and-hold investor is that if an investor was out of the market for just the twenty worst months when stocks were falling like a rock, his investment might be worth $1,760,000. Another Wall Street saying to remember is:

Investors can lose more money when stocks go down than they can make when they go up.

Because the average investor can lose more money when stocks go down than they can make when stocks go up, a buy-and-hold strategy may not be the best way to invest during prolonged bear markets, which have occurred over the past few years. In fact, a period of falling stock and mutual fund prices can reduce a buy-and-hold investor's annual returns over five years to less than those of a taxable money-market fund, and in many cases to an annual loss. As a result, individually managed accounts have become one of the fastest growing ways to invest.

Portfolio Investing

Your next step is to build a portfolio of stocks you can live with until you retire.

Trend 12 Portfolio

With portfolio manager Easan Katir, I've organized a portfolio of twelve stocks called the Trend 12 Portfolio as an alternative to a buy-and-hold approach. You may have heard Easan Katir interviewed on my radio show or seen him on CNBC television. He has many years experience in portfolio management in both London and the United States.

This portfolio is invested either in stocks or in cash. When the stock starts a downtrend, the stock is sold and the money is held in cash. When the stock rebounds and begins an uptrend, the stock is repurchased. Can a portfolio manager always sell at the top and buy at the bottom? As you will later learn, they cannot. But Easan Katir has read the stock charts for many years and has found that he can often buy at the beginning of an uptrend and sell when it ends. He says that each stock in the Trend 12 has a personality. Some prices move lethargically and some run up and down in share price with great emotion. The lesson I learned through following charts and selling on a downtrend and buying back the same shares on an upturn is that I've avoided much of the losses in a down market.

Look carefully at a chart of index prices and you will notice over the long term, the general trend of the indices is up. There are, however, periods of five to ten years along the way that are relatively flat. After the historic price moves of the nineties, we may have entered one of those periods.

During the nineties every other month seemed to bring a new high. In contrast, consider that the indices haven't made new highs for about two years now. Buying and holding the S&P 500 for the past two years has resulted in a return of around −20 percent. Not an encouraging period in one's investing life.

Trend Analysis of Charts

Here is how trend analysis works. Suppose there is a stock called ABC. Although it is a solid company, because of market conditions, economic conditions, antitrust concerns, the price of ABC begins the year at $100, drops to $50 in May, and rebounds to $100 by December. This type of volatility is not uncommon for even the bluest of blue chips, such as IBM, Merck, or Microsoft.

For a buy-and-hold investor, the return on ABC stock for the year is zero, along with a few sleepless summer nights. With trend analysis, a portfolio manager sees the price break the uptrend average price, and sells at $90. Then waits in cash for the uptrend to resume. There are sometimes false uptrends, so, for example, let's say the manager buys at $60, sells at $55 as the downtrend resumes. Then after some patience, the stock bottoms at $50 and the manager buys in the new uptrend at $60. There are sometimes corrections along the way, so he may sell at $70 in September, and buy back at $75 in October, ending the year at $100.

While the buy-and-hold investor has lost 50 points, then made 50 points, for a net return of zero, the trend investor has made 20 points in the same year. How is that? (100 − 90) − (60 − 55) + (70 − 60) + (100 − 75) = 20. He has been in cash during much of the downtrend, missing the worst days of the market, and back in stock when the uptrend resumes. Notice it is not assumed one sells at the exact high or buys at the exact low. Also, not every purchase and sale is profitable. Over time, trend analysis is a good way to make money and avoid losses in bear markets or up and down markets, such as we've been in for the past two years. Is this a lot of work? Yes, it is. Does it require constant vigilance and attention? Yes, it does. But if the portfolio manager can read the charts, sell when the stock is falling, wait for a market rebound and buy when the stock begins an uptrend, the returns can be substantially higher than a typical buy-and-hold portfolio.

In a recent real-life example, Easan sold GE from the Trend 12 portfolio on March 22, 2002, at $37 when the price closed below the uptrend line. He repurchased more shares of GE at $26 right after the July selling panic, and as of this writing the price is $30. So trend analysis saved the portfolio from a 30 percent loss as GE swooned from $37 to $26, and portfolio investors enjoyed a 15 percent profit from this stock's uptrend.

Another Kind of Compounding

In trend analysis investing, one can use a form of compounding that is generally not known. This occurs when 1,000 shares are sold at $90, as in our example above, and then when the price is $60, 1,500 shares of the same stock are purchased. So if the price returns to $100, the buy-and-hold investor has the same 1,000 shares, and the Trend 12 investor has 1,500 shares. When the share price of the stock later rises in an up market, the Trend 12 investor with 500 more shares will make substantial gains over the buy-and-hold investor. For example, if the price of $60 a share rises to $65 a share the buy-and-hold investor will make $5,000 on 1,000 shares. But the Trend 12 investor will make $7,500 on 1,500 shares.

Keeping tabs on a portfolio of stock trends every day is more work than most people have the time for or perhaps the experience to accomplish. I don't recommend you try this unless you are well schooled in trend analysis and chart pattern recognition. One way to do this is to employ a portfolio manager to keep track of the trends and authorize him to buy and sell as needed in these turbulent markets. He does this with a managed account.

Individually Managed Accounts

In the past wealthy investors who had upward of $500,000 could invest in separate managed accounts. Today, with computers and block trading, the minimum can be as low as $50,000. An individually managed account differs from a mutual fund in that the investors own the individual securities in their own account, rather than having an interest in an investment pooled mutual fund. Invested funds typically go into a brokerage account and the account is accessible at any time on the web or with monthly statements. Often the portfolio manager has discretionary authority within general guidelines. For instance, the investor could authorize the manager to invest in any of the Dow 30 stocks without discussing it first.

If at any time the investor needs cash, he or she can contact the brokerage firm and the cash can be quickly in their hands. Most individually managed accounts do not charge a load or a sales commission and there is no charge for withdrawals. Typically, there is an annual management fee paid monthly or quarterly.

Individually managed accounts offer several advantages over mutual funds. They generally provide better tax benefits, since investors are not subject to "phantom" capital gains as is possible in funds. They keep the risk level to the known securities in the account, and you don't have to worry about fund investors bailing out and the fund manager selling huge blocks of stock.

Mutual funds have been notorious for not disclosing their current assets or not letting investors see exactly what the fund manager is doing. The best most investors can do is to check with one of the fund services like Morningstar and look at the fund's top five holdings, which could be months old. With a managed account, the investor sees exactly which stocks are in his or her portfolio at any time.

This can be a bit nerve-racking if a portfolio manager is working diligently for performance. You never see all these behind-the-scenes activities in your mutual fund. The fund managers don't want investors to see the rough-and-tumble daily maneuvering to enhance performance. There would be too many queries from shareholders. There are various techniques with which the investor may not be familiar. For instance, if the account is large, the manager may scale into a position, buy a few shares, then more later. There may be a period of choppiness where trends are not clear, and the manager may buy only to sell a short time later as trends reverse. The stock market is sometimes fickle.

A noted portfolio manager was once asked how he was able to buy near the exact lows, and he replied that observers didn't always appreciate it was sometimes his fourth or fifth entry into the market, working hard to be in the uptrend if it was sustained, and preserve his clients' capital if it was not.

Investment managers will often use limit orders. When an investor buys a stock with a market order, he is paying the price of the stock when the order is executed. A fund manager will ascertain where the price of a stock he needs to buy is likely to retrace and place a limit order there, sometimes taking a few hours, days, or weeks to buy a stock at the optimum price. Sometimes this saves only a few dollars, but year in and year out, this adds up to additional portfolio profits.

Trend 12 Plus Portfolio

The Trend 12 Plus Portfolio, like the Trend 12, is invested in either the twelve stocks or cash. When a stock starts a downtrend, the stock is sold and the money is held in cash. When the stock rebounds and begins an uptrend, the stock is repurchased. In the past two years, however, this has resulted in large cash positions in the Trend 12 as the bear market pulled most stocks down in price. With interest rates around 2 percent, this cash is "dead money." The best news is that this is preserving one's nest egg during bad times, which, of course is better than losing it.

There is a method to actually profit from down moves in the market, which aggressive investors may want to consider. I call it the Trend 12 Plus. Even the best companies become overvalued or conditions change, and their share price could suffer. Consider IBM in the spring of 2002, which declined from $126 to $79 in a few months, a portfolio-rattling −38 percent. A money manager who studies the trends could be in a stock during an uptrend (a *long* position), and *sell short* a stock during a downtrend. The vast majority of mutual funds do not do this, but it can supercharge your portfolio.

Each investor should clearly understand the risks and rewards before deciding to authorize their money manager to employ this method.

What is *selling short*? In a nutshell, it means the portfolio makes money when a share price declines. The mechanics sound a little complicated, but in practice it is almost as easy for a manager to sell short as it is to purchase shares long.

The behind-the-scenes mechanics of the transaction are this: Say, for example, the manager sees signs of ABC beginning a downtrend. He puts in an order with the custodial broker to sell short 1,000 shares of ABC. The brokerage firm loans the account 1,000 shares and immediately sells them. On the account statement, it will say −1,000 ABC, plus the interest on the loan of the stock. If the expected price decline occurs, the manager puts in an order to *buy to cover* when the downtrends shows signs of ending. If, for example, the price of our hypothetical ABC declined to $60, and shares were purchased, it would close out the short position, and the 1,000 shares would be returned to the brokerage firm. The broker's back office computers do all this. It's not like returning your neighbor's lawn mower you borrowed. It's all very efficient. In this case, the profit would be the sale price, $90 a share, less the purchase price, $60 a share to return the shares you borrowed from the broker, for a $30-a-share profit. All while the buy-and-hold crowd are gritting their teeth.

What if the price goes up while a portfolio is short? Then the portfolio loses some money. For example, if one sold short at $90 and the price went to $95, the loss would be $5 a share.

There's some mystery about selling short, first because companies don't especially like investors hoping their stock price will decline, and second because of added risk. Usually a portfolio can only lose money when prices decline. With selling short, it is possible to lose money when prices go up.

There are misconceptions, though. The old canard one hears trotted out with every discussion of short sales is "a stock price can go to infinity." While theoretically that is true, it has never happened. A prudent manager will have a stop-loss order on a short position, to limit risk of loss. Saying a price can go to infinity is like saying a stock price can go to zero every time one purchases a stock. Again, that is theoretically true, but it almost never happens, and a prudent manager using trend analysis will have sold the position long before it does.

Still there is a bias toward the long side of stock ownership. Some managers just constitutionally can't bring themselves to sell short. Because of their background, it just is an uncomfortable feeling. Some trend analysts are good at spotting bottoming formations, so they know when to buy, but have trouble seeing top patterns, so are less comfortable selling short. Easan Katir, portfolio manager of Trend 12, says many of the patterns are the same. If one can see them on the lows but not on the highs, there is a simple solution to train one's eye. Turn the computer monitor upside down!

A Comparison of Buy and Hold and Trend Investing

To summarize, here is how the two investing methods would hypothetically work in three markets: an uptrending market, a choppy, trendless market, and a downtrending market.

Portfolio	Up	Choppy	Down
Trend 12	+15%	+10%	−5%
Trend 12 Plus	+15%	+15%	+10%

The Trend 12, catching the uptrends and avoiding downtrends, gains in uptrending or choppy markets, and loses less in a down market. The Trend 12 Plus, which seeks to profit in downtrends as well as uptrends, gains some in each of the three examples.

These examples are to display the principle of each portfolio's investment style. Actual results, of course, will vary, and as you can see from the down market column, there is no guarantee against loss in any stock market investment.

An investor should also consider expenses and taxes in gauging one's choice of investment methods. Individually managed accounts can incur short-term capital gains in an uptrending market, but it is better to pay taxes on profit than to lose principal in a down market. In a tax-qualified retirement plan, such as a IRA, 401(k), or other retirement plan, taxes can be deferred until withdrawal.

How to Manage Your Portfolio

Once you have established your portfolio, remember these basic rules:

Look at the stock market long-term

Risk from investing in the stock market must be viewed as an acceptable *long-term risk,* especially when you invest for retirement. From time to time the turbulence in the market may be giving you the jitters, but don't get distracted by short-term performance. The stock market's performance, as measured by the thirty stocks in the Dow Jones Industrial Average, closed at 9605 just before the September 11, 2001 terrorism attack. By January 1, 2002, the Dow was back to about 1050. By midyear, July 2002, the Dow had fallen to 9000, and in late July the market crashed to a lower level than the previous September 11 level, or 7700. No one can predict the future, of course, but if history is any gauge, the Dow Jones Industrials could be back over the previous high of 11,000 in early 2003.

Don't overdiversify

Fifteen stocks and three or four mutual funds is more than enough for the average investor. Those stocks can be in the sectors that have made the most money over the years and can be expected to make money in the next ten years: technology, pharmaceuticals, financials, and entertainment.

Don't tinker with your portfolio

In my Trend 12, I let the portfolio manager buy and sell the same stocks depending on their price movement. The long-term objective of any portfolio is to increase *total value,* not the performance of any particular stocks during any short-term period. Using trend analysis capitalizes on the price swings caused by market and industry trends. Look at Pfizer, it was up a whopping 67 percent in 1998, down 22 percent in 1999, and up 42 percent in 2000. This lesson tells us to be vigilant for trend changes. As much work as it seems, there is no substitute for a small portfolio of good stocks with a long-term view and diligent management.

Make regular investments

My father told me to invest in stocks every time I had some spare cash and forget about what people say the stock market will do. It cut my level of anxiety when I continued to invest in a falling stock market, and it gave me courage to continue investing when everyone else said I was crazy. It turned out my father was right.

Forget about your panic when the market takes a gut-wrenching nosedive (your stocks will cost less), or when the stock market is setting new records (your stocks will go up). Your job is always to invest on a regular schedule. For many people, starting an investment plan is the most difficult part of investing. They wonder when is the best time to invest? The answer is that *it doesn't make any difference!* Let's say you were a soothsayer who could outguess the market and you made a $5,000 investment in stocks each year for the past twenty years at the best possible time, when the stock market was at its low for the year. Now, let's say that I made the same investment at the worst possible time each year, when the stock market was at its highest point. Even if you could have picked the very best time each year to invest, researchers have found that you would have ended up twenty years later with less than 2 percent more than I had investing at the worst possible time each year.

Shoestring Investing

For most people heading into retirement there is only one thing that stands between them and a handsome stock and mutual fund portfolio: money. Here are some ways to start investing on a regular basis within anyone's budget.

Open a discount brokerage account

This will allow you, within an IRA or on your own, to buy a few shares of stock each month. You can check your portfolio's value on the web and you'll receive monthly statements of your account.

Buy stocks directly from a company

You can do this with a dividend reinvestment plan, or DRIP. Most of the blue-chip stocks or my favorites (but not all) can be purchased directly from the various individual companies with an initial investment of $100 to $250. Investors typically must buy at least one share, but then they can buy shares or fractions of shares for as little as $50 to $100 per month and avoid costly broker's fees, which are relatively higher the smaller the size of your trade. DRIP plans require an automatic investment plan, which is usually an automatic deduction from your checking account each month. Most companies that offer these plans offer IRAs, automatically reinvest your dividends, allow you to buy fractional shares of stock, and let you sell your shares with a phone call. About 1,300 companies offer stock directly to the public. To get started in direct purchase plans, call these companies and learn about their plans:

- IBM: 888-426-6700; $500 initial, then $50 minimum
- General Electric: 800-786-2543; $250 initial, then $10 minimum
- Merck: 888-291-3713; $350 initial, then $50 minimum
- Pfizer: 800-733-9393, $500 initial, and then $50 minimum

For more help, get The Drip Investor's 133-page *Directory of Dividend Reinvestment Plans.* You'll learn how to start investing in 1,100 companies with an initial investment of around $250. The directory costs $9.95 (plus $3.00 shipping). Call 800-233-5922, or log onto www.dripinvestor.com. Or write to Horizon Publishing Company, 7412 Calumet Avenue, Hammond, IN 46324. Or log onto www.netstockdirect.com for a list of companies that sell stock directly to the public.

Many people have also found that shoestring investing is a great way to build a stock portfolio for their kids or grandkids. You might buy McDonald's, Disney, and Microsoft and let the kids rip out the business section when they want to see the price of their stock.

Buy mutual funds on the cheap

Most mutual funds today require a $3,000 to $5,000 minimum investment to open a regular account (though $500 can usually open an IRA account). The good news is that you can invest in top-flight funds even with $50 a month if you agree to an automatic investment plan (a withdrawal each month from your checking account). Once you start the plan, however, you normally have to continue investing until you reach the fund's standard minimum investment amount.

The Mutual Fund Education Alliance, a trade group of mutual funds, has a list of excellent funds that allow as little as a $50-a-month investment. On the internet, log onto www.mfea.com for a list and how to invest.

Dollar Cost Averaging. This time-honored technique allows any investor to tiptoe into the stock market by investing a fixed amount of money at regular intervals. Many mutual funds, such as Vanguard Funds, will help you set up dollar-cost-averaging arrangements and make automatic transfers from your bank account to various funds.

The idea behind dollar cost averaging is that you are not only forced to invest regularly, but since you buy shares at different prices over time, you tend to average out the cost.

Let's suppose that you can invest $100 a month in the ABC Fund. In the first month, if ABC's shares were selling at $10, you would buy ten shares. If the price rises to $12.50 a share in the next month; you'd buy eight shares. The next month, ABC Fund's share price is back at $10 a share, and you would buy ten shares. Then, in the fourth month, ABC shares fall to $7.69 a share and you would buy 13 shares. In the fifth month, ABC Fund is back at $10 a share and you would buy ten shares. In the five-month period, you invested a total of $500 and you purchased fifty-one shares with an average cost of $9.80.

The advantage of dollar cost averaging is that not only do you continue to invest each month to build up your nest egg, but also the average cost per share can be lower than the average price per share. This example of dollar cost averaging will give you a general idea of how it works, even though the average mutual fund or stock share price may change less from month to month.

Why Not Invest in Mutual Funds?

It's as if mutual fund investors have traveled a long and twisting road the past few years and wound up either back where they started, or in many cases in the tech, dot-com, and global sectors, deep in the red.

With something over 4,000 stock funds, searching for the next superstar fund is like trying to find a needle in a haystack. The needle is buried in thousands of funds, but it's almost impossible to find.

A mutual fund is a basket of securities—stocks, bonds, or other securities—and investors don't own the securities in the basket directly, but instead buy or sell shares in the fund. Like most investments, the key points to consider are risk, return, and cost. Returns are often beyond your control, but you can tend to hold down risk and cost.

Typically, risks tend to mount when you invest in a certain industry or technology sector. The nation's largest fund, in terms of total dollars invested, the Standard & Poor's 500 stock index fund, might involve the least risk of all. This fund invests in 500 stocks, from very large to midsize companies in eight industry areas, and represents almost the entire stock market.

Another risk investing in mutual funds is the recent trend of *vanishing stock funds.* According to *USA Today* (September 9, 2002), almost 1,000 stock funds have either been liquidated or merged into the fund management's other funds since March 2000. If you are a shareholder in a mutual fund and the fund company folds one of these turkeys into your fund, you get stuck with all the failed fund's holdings.

But over the past few years the biggest problem for fund investors has been that *buying mutual funds comes without advice on when to sell.* The fund companies are unlikely to call you and tell you their fund is going into the tank, and the broker or planner has probably already forgotten you socked your money into the fund. This is truly "do-it-yourself" investing.

For many investors, however, mutual funds do offer instant diversification. If you have a few dollars to invest, it's better to be in a fund of several hundred stocks than just a few. The price you pay is that a fund invested in several hundred stocks *is the market* and investors typically earn the overall market rate of return, or less.

To be a successful mutual fund investor you need to ask the following questions before you invest:

- Is the fund no-load (without sales commissions), low-load (usually about 3 percent of purchase price), regular load (anywhere from 4 percent to 5.75 percent of the purchase price), or back-end load (a no-load fund where early surrender charges can be as high as 5 percent and decline each year, usually for up to three or four years after purchase). Some mutual funds also have an early withdrawal fee to discourage short-term traders. The exit fee can apply if you sell within three to six months after you purchased the fund.
- Does the fund have Class A shares with a front-end load at time of purchase, Class B shares with a deferred sales load for early surrender, or Class C with level 12b-1 charges each year for the life of the fund to help pay the fund's sales and marketing costs?
- What are the fund's annual management fees, 12b-1 fees, and other charges? You should be told the expenses a typical investor would pay on a $1,000 investment in the fund for one, three, five, and ten years before you invest.
- Is the fund a no-load, low-load, regular-load or back-end load? Does the fund charge a sales commission when you reinvest the dividends? Is there an early withdrawal fee if you sell within three or six months after you invest?
- Does the fund have Class A shares (front-end load), Class B (deferred back-end surrender charge), and Class C (level load of 12b-1 charges)? Are the sales charges, if any, reflected in the performance numbers?

- What are the fund's annual management fees, 12b-1 fees, and other charges? You should be told the expenses a typical investor would pay on a $1,000 investment for one, three, five, and ten years.
- What is the fund's turnover rate? The turnover rate tells you how frequently the fund sells the stocks in its portfolio. If you hold the funds outside a tax-qualified retirement plan, each time the fund sells a security within one year of purchase, the profits are taxed to you as ordinary income. Investments held for over one year are taxed at the lower capital gains rate. The twelve-month average turnover of managed mutual fund portfolios has soared to 90 percent, up from only 20 percent thirty years ago.
- What are the fund's possible risks and goals and who manages the fund?
- What kinds of securities does the fund invest in, and what amount does it already have in each category? If the fund calls itself a government securities fund, for example, what percentage of its assets are actually invested in government bonds?
- What is the minimum initial investment and minimum additional investment and what are the restrictions and costs, if any, for redeeming shares?
- What is the total return of the fund year to date at the time you plan to buy the fund and over the past three and five years, and how does the fund's performance over this same period compare to the total return of the Standard & Poor's 500 stock index?

Selecting Your Mutual Funds

The Olympics attract the best athletes in the world. But to make the team, they must prove that they can outperform the competition. If you are going to invest in a mutual fund, it should also be a medal winner and outperform the competition. The problem is that most funds don't even beat the market averages. In fact, Burton Malkiel, author of the investment classic *A Random Walk Down Wall Street,* believes that "the usefulness of trying to pick winning mutual funds run by genius managers is just about zero."

Each month the leading money magazines try to seduce you with a never-ending array of funds to buy now! Each of the funds is managed by a wizard of Wall Street who is sure to take your money and outguess the market. These high-priced fund managers face two major problems that make it very difficult for them to match the performance of non-managed index funds.

First, the portfolio mangers have to pick stocks that go up in price to provide the performance levels investors expect. The results of stock picking, however, have often been less than if the fund manger bought the entire stock market, turned out the lights, and simply went home.

Peter Lynch, who set performance records year after year when he was the portfolio manager of Fidelity's Magellan Fund, may have said it best: "Trying to time the market is a waste of time. I don't know anyone who has been right more than once in a row." Or, to put it another way, to buy and sell stocks at just the right time a portfolio manager would have to be right over 65 percent of the time just to break even on his or her trades. Only a few lucky traders can do this for any length of time.

Second, actively managed funds have to cover the costs of management, trading, and salaries that weigh down the fund's results. For example, the average mutual fund can have a 1.60 percent annual management fee, compared to an unmanaged S&P 500 stock index fund's average of around 0.20 percent. When a managed fund starts out with at least a 1.40 percent disadvantage, it's hard to outperform an index fund. Also, since index funds rarely trade stocks, they save on trading costs, and if an investor does not hold the fund in an IRA or 401(k)-type retirement plan, they can sharply cut the taxes due on the capital gains distributions each year.

One way to beat the odds, whether you're a beginning investor or a pro, is to simply take the no-brainer way investing in the stock market and earn the averages in index funds. Index investing works like this: You simply choose an index—made up of stocks, bonds, or other securities—and your return is the overall gain or loss of the entire index. For the average investor, index investing can allow broad diversification. An index can be the 30 stocks in the Dow Jones Industrial Average, the Standard & Poor's 500 stock index, the S&P midcap or S&P small-cap index, the Russell 3000, which represents 98 percent of the total equity market, or even the Wilshire 5000, which includes almost every publicly traded stock in the U.S.

George Sauter, the index manager for the Vanguard Mutual Fund group, whose Standard & Poor's 500 stock index fund is now the largest mutual fund in America, summed up index investing this way: "With index funds you won't have a chance of being number one in any given year, but you'll have a very good chance of being in the top 10 to 15 percent of all funds year in and year out. Investing in index funds," he says, "can be very boring, but you can count your money all the way to the bank."

John Bogle, founder and chairman of the Vanguard Group of funds, in his book *John Bogle on Investing: The First 50 Years* (McGraw Hill, 2000), told our radio listeners that "finding a good mutual fund is as straightforward as it is simple: Stop trying to find the needle. Invest in the haystack. Own the entire U.S. stock market. Today, that is as easily said as done."

Bogle believes the non-managed index funds offer many advantages:

- No sales commissions
- Always 100 percent invested in securities
- No (or only minimal) transaction cost, since stocks are held essentially forever
- Low taxes since stocks are seldom sold and incur capital gains taxes

John Bogle says, "To make a long story short, the stock market's annual return has averaged 16.9 percent during the past fifteen years. The average fund, net of its costs and taxes, earned an annual return of just 11.2 percent. A no-load, low turnover, low-cost all-market index fund, after its estimated and taxes, would have earned a return of 15.8 percent, a truly staggering enhancement of 4.6 percentage points per year." This difference, Bogle says, "compounded has a staggering impact on capital accumulation. Assuming an investment of $10,000 in 1984, the value of the average equity managed stock fund in late 1999, after costs and taxes, was $49,000. The final value in the all market index fund would have been $90,000."

It should come as no surprise that over the years, the S&P 500 index funds have consistently beaten the performance of all but a few of the managed mutual funds. According to Morningstar, the Chicago firm that tracks mutual funds (www.morningstar.com), as of May 1999, 89 percent of actively managed U.S. diversified equity funds trailed the S&P 500 stock index over the trailing ten-year period. As of the middle of 2000, the S&P 500 index had a five-year total return (with dividends reinvested) of 183 percent; the average large company stock fund made a return of 140 percent. Over a ten-year period, the S&P 500 index had a total return of 423 percent; the average large-company stock fund, only 348 percent.

If you want to diversity, you might invest in a small-cap or a midcap index fund and an index bond fund, and then put at least half your money into the S&P 500 index fund and the other half distributed in the small-cap and midcap funds and a bond fund.

Sector Funds

If imitation is the sincerest form of flattery, then the hottest funds today are the sector funds. The purpose of a sector fund is to invest in a major industry group, such as science and technology, health and biotechnology, gold and precious metals, financial services, or Internet stocks. The problem with sector funds is that you need to invest in several funds to diversify your holdings, and it's much more difficult to figure out whether an entire sector will do well than it is with a single stock.

It's also a waste of money to chase what appears at the time a hot fund. Usually, by the time the average investor buys a hot sector fund it's overvalued, leaving him to eat big losses when the sector eventually plummets.

You also need to watch out for portfolio managers who want to juice up the sector fund's performance numbers to attract more investors. One way is to use leverage (borrowing money to buy stocks). Surprised investors have found that while leveraging can magnify returns on the upside, they can also cause huge losses on the downside when the market turns against a sector.

If you want to build a portfolio of sector funds you might start with funds that invest in the drug, financial, and technology sectors. In any event, I would not put more than 10 percent of my assets in sector funds because, based on experience, they can go out of favor in a flash, and when they do, the same investors who were attracted by their great earlier returns will be the first to bail out of the fund. Since most of the fund's assets are invested in stocks, raising the cash to pay off departing shareholders could mean selling huge chunks of stocks at a loss, further depressing the fund's returns. The investors who remain in the fund are left holding the bag as redemptions create a downward spiraling of the fund's share price.

Asset Allocation

Now we come to the big enchilada, the most important investment strategy anyone can use. Why? Because studies by big pension fund managers, who manage billions of dollars, have found:

Over time, proper asset allocation can account for as much as 94 percent of your future gains.

In comparison, the same studies have shown that only slightly more than 2 percent of your investment gains come from individual stock and bond selection, less than 2 percent from buying and selling stock at just the right time, and about 2 percent are the result of all other factors.

Why should you remember this golden rule of asset allocation? Because after almost four decades of financial planning I know the increased returns you can earn each year with proper asset allocation are crucial. They can make the difference between a retirement in which you have to continue to work or one in which you spend your later years on the golf course or traveling in Europe.

The classic definition of asset allocation is the process of developing a diversified investment portfolio by mixing different assets in varying proportions. In other words: *Don't put all your eggs in one basket.*

The rule of thumb in asset allocation has been to have *at least* 100 minus your age in stocks or stock funds. If you are age 40, then at least 60 percent of your assets should be in stocks. Using this formula, the older you are, the less you'd have of your assets in equities and the more you'd have in income-producing bonds or fixed savings.

The biggest asset allocation mistakes investors make in their long-term financial planning is to put all or most of their money to work in short-term fixed savings, seeking safety of principal. Unless you are retired and need the interest income for living expenses or are saving for a short-term goal, keep your super-safe investments to a minimum.

Again, look at the numbers. If you made a one-time investment of $10,000 and you were 100 percent invested in bonds with the average annual return of 6.64 percent (let's call that 6.5 percent), or you were 100 percent invested in stocks with the average annual return of 14.8 percent (15 percent), you can see how asset allocation affects your total investment returns over time.

A One-time Investment of $10,000

Years Invested	100% Bonds @ 6.5%	100% stocks @ 15%
10	$18,770	$40,460
20	35,240	163,700
25	48,300	328,600

If you've invested in the safety of bonds, you've been wearing worn-out shoes. If you invested in stocks, you're slipping into a top-of-the-line Porsche. We're talking about how you'll live the rest of your life once you cash in your chips and retire. If you look closely at this chart, you'll see that over the first ten years, you can typically earn more that twice as much in stocks as you can in bonds. In twenty years, you can earn almost five times more, and in twenty-five years about seven times as much.

Or, to put it another way, after twenty-five years the $48,300 in bonds invested at 7 percent could provide an annual income of

$3,380; while the $328,600 that could be in the stock account would provide an annual income of $23,000. While this is not big money to Warren Buffett, to most people almost two grand a month is better than $280 a month to pay the rent.

If you remember nothing else from this book, remember this golden rule:

Proper asset allocation will likely account for as much as 94 percent of your future investment gain.

Do bonds have a place in your investment portfolio? Yes. It's always good to have about 5 or 10 percent of your assets in fixed-income bonds because:

- They tend to be less volatile than stocks, and that's a good thing if you are near or in retirement.
- They give you a pool of money to make withdrawals from when the bear market takes stocks down sharply. If you can live off this pool of money you won't have to sell some of your stocks or funds at bargain-basement prices, and you'll have the option of investing fresh cash in the beaten-down prices of stocks you already own.

Jorgensen's Model Portfolio

This is the investment plan I use in my seminars and it is only a base to work from depending on your individual situation. But I believe it can be a sound overall investment program for all most any investor.

10 percent in government bonds. Typically a no-load low-cost bond fund with free check-writing privileges for checks over $500.

20 percent in an S&P 500 stock index fund. A no-load index fund with a very low annual management fee.

60 percent in blue-chip (favorite) stocks. This could include investing with a discount broker or directly with the company. You might put equal amounts in each of the following stocks: GE, Coca-Cola, Microsoft, Johnson & Johnson, Intel, Exxon/Mobil, and IBM.

10 percent in cash or money-market account. This can provide a safety fund if you need cash without selling stocks in a down market, or as an opportunity investment fund.

If you are fascinated by all of this, you should be. Moreover, once you keep most of your money in stocks and stock mutual funds, maybe the dance on Wall Street will come into better focus as you come to understand why some people retire rich and others are never able to financially retire at all.

STEP 7

Delay Your Taxes

We cannot know where we are going, any of us, until we know where we have been and where we now find ourselves.

This English proverb may be as relevant today as it was when Richard II nailed it to the wall of Winchester Church in 1386. In short, if you don't know where you are going with your employer-sponsored retirement plan today, you can end up in a dead end street with no reverse gear. Before you crash into the wall, you could discover that "pension erasers" have stolen all of your employer's prior contributions and your comfortable retirement nest egg is almost gone.

Despite all of today's uncertainties, however, it is possible to develop strategies for a successful retirement. You need to consider that people are living longer and often retiring younger, so it's more important than ever that you make the necessary financial plans early in life. Charles Kettering, the head of research at General Motors, may have summed up retirement best when he said,

"We should all be concerned about the future because we will have to spend the rest of our lives there."

A recent survey of retired individuals asked, "If you had it to do over again, what would you do differently in planning for your retirement?" The answers at the top of the list were:

1. Would have planned much earlier; never thought about getting old.
2. Would have saved more money from each paycheck and made better investments.
3. Would have bought a home.
4. Would have worked harder to get a better education; would have continued education.
5. Would have bought more life insurance.

How Our Retirement System Has Changed

Over the past decade company-paid pensions have been in retreat. One reason is that employers discovered that with rising inflation, salaries on which retirement benefits were based were soaring. To keep a pension plan in place the companies needed to continually force-feed a cash-hungry pension system to meet the ever-higher monthly retirement checks promised to employees in the contract. The other reason was that retirees were living longer and collecting a lot more retirement checks. In 1946, life expectancy at age 65 was only 13.5 years. Today, it's about 19 years. On average that's 66 more inflation-bloated monthly benefits checks per retiree than pension managers estimated they would need when they set up the plan.

The answer for most companies has been to switch to a 401(k) contribution plan that takes the employer off the hook for any promised future benefits and lets employees share in the cost of their retirement.

As a result, the decline in company-paid pension benefits has become the biggest factor in the reduction of workers' retirement security. A March 26, 2001, *USA Today* article reported that in 1992, 21.5 percent of U.S. families had a 401(k), and 22.6 percent had a pension. By 1995, 29.4 percent had a 401(k), but those who also had a pension fell to 14.3 percent. By 1998, 32.6 percent of these families had a 401(k) plan, but only 11.3 percent were also covered under a pension plan.

More workers are covered by retirement plans that require them to make contributions, or are not covered at all, than are covered by company-paid pension plans.

Before your 401(k) becomes a 201(k) and your retirement plans go into the Dumpster, it could help if you understand your basic retirement plan choices.

Defined Benefit Pension Plan

Although many company retirement plans are referred to as pensions, most of today's workforce isn't covered by a pension. The word *defined* comes from the fact that the benefit at retirement is defined in advance. The pension benefit is typically based on the average of the employee's last five years' salary, the number of years of service with the employer, and the age at retirement. Often half of the pension benefits can accrue in the last five or ten years of service.

In order to meet the terms of the pension, the company must annually contribute the amount required to support the pension fund's stated benefits. If an employee leaves early, however, the sum in his or her account that is not vested could revert to the company to cut future pension payins.

Because of the increased cost of defined benefit pensions, many retirees find they are covered by a phantom pension fund. One reason is the *break-in-service* provision, which sharply reduces pension benefits if the employee leaves the company and then later returns. With today's job hoppers, this provision has been a nightmare. Under the Employment Retirement Income Security Act, or Erisa, returning employees must be given credit for previous years of service, or be allowed to buy them back.

If, however, the departing employee takes a cash payout of the vested fund balance (and most do) and then returns to the company without repaying the money, the amount withdrawn is deducted from his or her pension account. What many returning employees do not realize is that the unreturned withdrawal is placed in a phantom account and on paper grows at a very high rate. At retirement, this huge phantom account is deducted from the actual pension account, substantially reducing the monthly pension benefits.

Pension Benefit Guaranty Corporation (PBGC)

This government agency insures private and nonprofit pension plans in the event the company terminates the plan or files for bankruptcy. To be included in the insurance program, companies generally need to have a large number of employees and pay the insurance premiums to the PBGC. As more and more employees were forced to draw these benefits, insurance premiums have soared. Benefits at age 65 are generally about two-thirds of what a typical private pension plan might pay with limits on monthly benefits.

For more information contact: PBGC 1200 K Street, NW, Suite 930, Washington, DC 20005-4026, 202-326-4000.

Cash Balance Plans

The newest twist to cut pension costs is the *cash-balance pension plan.* With this plan a company can typically avoid any future commitments to a guaranteed pension benefit by contributing the equivalent of 4 percent to 7 percent of pay, based on the level of salary, into an account for each employee.

Companies say these new plans reflect the changing workforce and are necessary to attract mobile younger workers who care more about building assets now than about far-off pension benefits. As a result, the cash-balance plans can be portable and follow a job-hopping employee from job to job. When an employee leaves the employer's plan, depending on their vesting in the plan, they generally take a lump-sum payout from the cash-balance plan. The payout can be rolled over to an IRA or taken as cash.

What employers don't say is that the new cash-balance plans are big cost-cutters over defined-benefit pension plans. The savings results from the fact that the small average yearly contributions made for each employee enables a company to avoid the very expensive defined benefit pension funding for long-time employees with high salaries near retirement age. As a result, younger workers score big under cash-benefits plans. A typical person who works for a company for more than five years and quits at age 31 could have a portable pension benefit worth 37 percent of his or her final pay, but only 7 percent in a traditional defined benefit pension. A typical worker who left a company at age 61 would have about 147 percent of his or her final pay under a cash-balance plan, but 213 percent under a traditional pension.

The longtime employee is the loser when a company shifts from a traditional to a cash-balance plan. As newcomers to the workforce, they were covered by a traditional pension plan that put younger workers at a disadvantage; as they near retirement, the new cash-balance plan puts them right back at the bottom of the totem pole.

Defined Contribution Plans

The employer's only obligation under this plan is to make a defined contribution for each covered worker. Since these contributions must be made each year regardless of profits, the number of these plans is rapidly decreasing. Defined-contribution plans differ from defined-benefit plans because the employer offers no guaranteed benefits at retirement. They are often referred to as *money purchase plans* because the retirement benefit is whatever the assets in the plan will purchase at the employee's retirement.

Profit-Sharing Plans

These plans make it even easier for a company to offer retirement plans. Since the obligation is to make contributions only in those years the company makes a profit, these plans are often more illusion than reality. What's more, the company can change the rate of contributions or eliminate them in any year. Like a money purchase plan, the retirement benefits are whatever the assets in the employee's account will purchase at retirement.

Employee Stock Ownership Plans (ESOPs)

Under this plan, the company makes contributions to employee retirement plans in the form of company stock. Employees may also make their own contributions to purchase additional shares of company stock through payroll deductions. Typically, the employee must contribute a certain percentage of pay to the plan before the employer will match with company stock. ESOPs are a form of profit sharing, and employee stock purchases are made with before-tax dollars. Any gain in the price of the stock is not taxed until the stock is withdrawn from the plan and sold.

Consider participating in an ESOP only if you believe that your company has good long-term prospects. If you do participate, consider investing only a third of your retirement contributions in company stock. The risk in an ESOP is that if the price of the company's stock declines significantly, you could take a big loss on a major portion of your retirement nest egg.

403(b) Plans

How did the brass ring of all employer-sponsored retirement plans come about? In the 1950s, teachers and workers at private non-profit organizations such as hospitals and charitable foundations did not have company-sponsored retirement plans, or participate in Social Security. As a result, Congress passed the Technical Amendments Law of 1958, then in 1961 amended the original section of the act and created 403(b) accounts.

Often referred to as tax-sheltered annuities (TSAs), the plans work much like any other employer-sponsored retirement plan, expect those covered under the plan get juicy options that most of us can only dream about. You can invest in a fixed or variable insurance company annuity, known as a 403(b) I account, or in mutual funds, known as a 403(b)7 account. After termination of current employment, 403(b) plans can be transfered from one 403(b) to another or into an IRA. IRA funds, however, can't be rolled over into a 403(b) plan unless they originally came from a 403(b) plan. Withdrawal requirements are the same as for any other tax-qualified plan.

You can also borrow from the plan for any reason. You generally can borrow 100 percent of the first $10,000 of the account value from insurance products. Loans are not permitted for the next $10,000, but you may borrow 50 percent of account values above $20,000, not to exceed $50,000. Non-real-estate loans must be paid back within five years, but home mortgage loans may be for as long as thirty years. The 403(b)7 mutual fund accounts may only loan 50 percent of the account value, not to exceed $50,000.

Worker contribution limits make the 403(b) plans shine. Unlike an IRA or other plans, you can contribute up to 20 percent of your salary into a 403(b) plan, not to exceed $11,000 in 2002, increasing to $15,000 by 2005. With a $3,000 annual cap on an IRA, these limits are spicy prospects indeed. But the big payoff comes when your kids are grown and you have more income to sock away. With the 403(b) *catch-up clause,* you can turn back the clock and make up for years when little or no contributions were made. Put the catch-up and regular contribution limits together and you can end up in your later years with a huge chunk of your monthly salary going into this gold-plated retirement plan.

Log onto www.403bwise.com for more information on contributions and withdrawls permitted under the latest tax laws.

401(k) Plans

Named after the section in the Internal Revenue Code that sanctioned them in 1978, 401(k) plans are the fastest growing employer-sponsored retirement plan. About 42 million workers have $1.8 trillion in assets in 401(k) plans. To encourage more employees to sign up and make payroll deductions into their 401(k) plans, some employers now offer eligibility after only three months on the job instead of the typical one-year wait. Many other employers have adopted automatic enrollment. Under this plan, employees are signed up unless they specifically choose not to be.

As of 2002, employees can stash as much as $11,000 in a 401(k), then, increasing $1,000 annually, $15,000 in 2006. Employees who reach age 50 before year-end can increase these limits by $1,000 in 2002, with a limit on catch-up contributions of $5,000.

At one time the company paid the fees to maintain the employer-sponsored retirement plans. Today as many as 40 percent of the companies with 401(k) plans charge employees record-keeping fees, and many charge a trustee fee to keep custody of the plan assets. Annual fees below 1 percent are reasonable, but some fees have run to more than 2 percent. It may be difficult for you to find out what retirement plan fees you are paying, as many companies only disclose these fees upon written request.

Employer Contributions

A letter outlining one company's matching program for its 401(k) plan put it this way: "The company is making it clear that employees must take responsibility for a share of their own retirement security." Many employers require a worker to first make voluntary contributions from his or her paycheck before the company will kick in any money.

Typically, these plans provide employer matches of from 25 or 50 cents to a dollar for every dollar of employee contributions, up to 5 or 6 percent of pay. In one plan, the employer matches employee contributions dollar for dollar on the first 3 percent of pay and 50 cents on the dollar for the next 2 percent of pay. Under other plans, the employee has to set aside at least 5 percent of pay to trigger the maximum match. Most 401(k) plans also allow employees the opportunity to make additional contributions on their own.

Suppose you contribute $3,000 a year from your salary and your employer matches your contribution 50 cents on the dollar. The following chart illustrates the benefits you could receive with matched contributions, compared to an investment made outside the 401(k) plan.

One-Year Growth Comparison

	401(k)	Non-Retirement Plan
Amount saved	$3,000	$3,000
Less taxes @ 30%	0	(900)
Amount invested, with 50% match	4,500	2,100
Earnings, 1st year @ 10%	450	210
Less taxes @ 30%	0	63
Balance year end	$4,950	$2,247

This is not a figment of your imagination. In the first year, with a 50 cents on the dollar match, you actually save $3,000 from your paycheck and end up with almost $5,000!

Five-Year Growth Comparison

	401(k)	Non-Retirement Plan
Total amount saved	$15,000	$15,000
Less taxes @ 30%	0	(4,500)
Amount invested, with 50% match	22,500	10,500
Balance after five years	$30,220	$12,920

Look at the numbers again. You have payroll deductions of $3,000 a year from your paycheck for five years, yet each year, on average, your retirement nest egg increases $6,000 a year. I know you are thinking it's too good to be true. Well, I should add that taxes have to be paid on the 401(k) money when you eventually withdraw the funds. However, under this example, if you are in a 30 percent state and federal income tax bracket, and if you withdrew all the money, you would have about $21,000 after taxes from the 401(k) plan, and only about $13,000 from your own investments. In retirement, you may be in a lower tax bracket, and the amount you pull out of your 401(k) account after taxes could be even larger.

If you can continue this plan for the next fifteen years, the numbers get even better. With your annual contribution, including the company's match, and assuming you can earn the long-time stock market average of 13 percent a year, you could end up with a $205,000 nest egg. In twenty years, the total could be as much as $415,000. Then if you retire and don't need this nest egg for only five more years, and you continue to earn the 13 percent without further contributions, you could be looking at about $764,000!

Vesting

Like a magician's vanishing act, a good part of your retirement plan assets can disappear even before you collect them.

What you are about to read is not found in most personal finance books. In fact, most people don't know the inner workings of a company-sponsored retirement plan until the fine print bites them, and then it is too late to back up and start over.

"Take this job and get our super retirement plan," the employment offer screams. You look at the plan and it is indeed a very rich plan that could put you on Easy Street when you retire. But more and more job switchers are finding that matching funds they thought were flowing into their retirement accounts don't follow them out the door when they leave.

If you plan to change jobs (or are let go), try to plan as far in advance as you can so you won't be ripped off when you leave your employer. It's not that you shouldn't consider changing jobs; the bright lights of new opportunities often shine brilliantly and lead the way to new advancements in job satisfaction and income. What you have to do is plan carefully so that you can take as much of your employer's contributions to your retirement plan with you as possible. We're not talking about nickels and dimes. You can easily lose $50,000 or more if you're not paying close attention.

Some employers will try to talk you into leaving your money in the retirement plan until you retire, offering to pay you a monthly income when you reach the plan's retirement age. This may sound like a good idea, but remember, if you can get your hands on the money from your employer's plan when you leave instead of waiting for a monthly pension, you'll accomplish three important things:

- You won't have to locate the company's retirement plan some fifteen to twenty years down the road.
- You'll be able to manage your own money without the restrictions and limitations of the employer's plan.
- You won't have to take a fixed (usually without indexing for inflation) monthly pension payout the plan offers.

Vesting is one of the magic words in retirement plans. It tells you how much of your previous employer's contributions you can take with you if you leave your job, are laid off, or retire. All of your own prior contributions, and the earnings on them, will be returned to you, but the vesting schedule determines your total payout.

Vesting schedules vary among employers. Typically, you are fully vested if you die or become totally and permanently disabled. If you are unsure of your vesting schedule or want to learn more about your company's retirement plan, ask your employer for a copy of its "Summary Plan Description" booklet. Here are two typical vesting schedules:

- **100 percent vested upon completion of three years of service in the plan.** You start the clock when you become eligible for coverage in the company retirement plan, not when you joined the company. If you leave before three years in the plan, you would have zero vesting.
- **20 percent vested each year beginning with the second year in the plan and ending with 100 percent vesting after six years of service.** For example, if you left the job after four years you would get 60 percent; with six or more years you could take 100 percent of the employer's contributions and the earnings.

This vesting schedule can bite job hoppers in the wallet. Considering the U.S. Department of Labor's recent report that workers age 25 to 35 stay on a job on average only 2.6 years, millions of departing employees are watching big chunks of their expected retirement nest egg vanish. Please check the vesting schedule in your company plan. If you plan to leave your current job and it's possible to stay beyond another plan anniversary date, you might take a big chunk of money you would otherwise kiss good-bye.

Borrowing from Your Company Retirement Plan

Almost two-thirds of employers who offer company retirement plans such as 401(k)s allow employees to borrow their own money from the plan. Generally, you can borrow half your vested account balance, up to a maximum of $50,000. While there is no required minimum, most companies set minimum loans from $500 to $1,000. Since this is a loan, the money you take out of your retirement plan is not taxable income, and if you are under the age of 59½, you are not subject to the 10 percent early withdrawal penalty.

Borrowing from the plan is usually permitted for emergency medical expenses, "hardships," and college costs. For someone buying his or her first home, borrowing the money from their 401(k) account for the down payment could be very attractive. This is the fastest way I know to save for the down payment on a tax-free basis. On the other hand, if you already own a home, a home-equity loan is a better deal since you can deduct the interest and the rates are about the same.

Most retirement plan loans are repaid though payroll deduction for a term of five to ten years. If you use the money to buy a primary home, you might be able to take as long as fifteen to twenty years to repay the loan. The kicker in becoming your own bank is that if you leave your job, the entire loan can become due and payable. If that happens, you have two choices. You can find the money to pay off the loan and roll over your entire retirement plan account to an IRA. If you can't repay the loan, the unpaid amount will be considered a taxable lump-sum distribution from the plan. If you are under the age of 59½, you could also face a 10 percent early withdrawal tax penalty. Sometimes another option is available to you—you can ask your old employer to keep your plan open and you can continue to make monthly contributions to the outstanding loan.

When You Leave Your Job

If you leave your job for any reason, chances are your employer will say, in effect, "Here's your retirement plan; come and get it." What the employer will offer you is a lump-sum distribution of the entire account. This will include your own contributions and the earnings on them and any fully vested employer contributions and earnings you have in the plan.

If your account balance is less than $5,000, your former employer can cash you out of the plan. This will force you either to roll over the assets into an IRA or to take the cash—and pay taxes on it. If the amount is over $5,000, you can leave the money in the plan, even if you decide to enroll in a new employer's plan. If you withdraw the money, you have the following options.

Take the money and run

Like carnival mirrors that make people look overly tall or wide, focusing on the money alone and what it will buy today is taking a shortsighted view of the situation. To make it simple: You can't get rich if you give your money away to Uncle Sam. Unfortunately, this has become the option of choice for job hoppers. According to a 1999 study by Hewitt Associates, a management consulting firm, of 170,000 distributions, 68 percent of plan participants opted for cash when changing jobs. You read that last sentence correctly. The majority of 401(k) plan participants who changed jobs regardless of age chose to take lump-sum cash payments. Anyone under age 59½ who did so also saw the value of their funds shrink about 45 percent with taxes and penalties.

Never take the cash and run.

We already know that only a few people retire rich. Those who do are more than likely the ones that took advantage of the power of compound interest. In other words, they kept their hands off those funds. Look at the numbers: Say you have $15,000 in your company retirement plan. If you are under the age of 59½ and you grab the cash, the government's haircut can leave you with about $9,000 in your pocket.

Now let's say you rolled over the $15,000 into an IRA and invested in an equity mutual fund. If you take Warren Buffett's advice and hold on to your investments, and you earn the average stock market return of 13 percent each year, the magic of compounding will take the $15,000 and turn it into almost $100,000 in fifteen years. Give the fund another five years and it could put

$173,000 in your retirement nest egg. In twenty-five years the account could be worth about $320,000! That's a cool third of a million during your working lifetime on just a $15,000 down payment!

Take the money and retire

You can take out as much money as you want without paying the 10 percent early withdrawal penalty, as long as you meet these conditions:

- You are at least age 55.
- You have a retirement plan with your employer, such as a 401(k), 403(b), or ESOP plan. This option is not available for IRAs.
- You leave your job or a have a *separation of service* as defined by the IRS. You can later go to work for another company or even your prior employer.

Under this rule, you can make as many penalty-free withdrawals as you like from your employer-sponsored plan before age 59½, but once you roll over the money to an IRA, you lose this option.

If you were born before 1936: You may take "income averaging" on withdrawals (and possibly the lower capital gains tax rate for pre-1974 participation). This can substantially reduce your taxes on withdrawals. See your accounting or financial advisor if you qualify.

Keep the money in your former employer's plan

Some people believe that their former employer can manage their money better than they can. If your prior employer permits, you can leave your retirement plan money with the company. You can always ask for a lump-sum distribution later on and spend the money or roll it over into an IRA.

Take the money and then decide to roll it over to an IRA

In this case, since you have your hands on the money (less 20 percent withholding), you will have to come up with the missing 20 percent to make the full rollover to an IRA, and then file for a refund on your next tax return. If you fail to come up with the cash to replace the money withheld by the employer for taxes, the money will be considered an early withdrawal and subject to regular income taxes.

Roll over the money directly into an IRA

Under current rules, it's important that you have an established IRA to receive the money. That way the company can send the money directly to your IRA trustee and you'll avoid the 20 percent withholding in a tax-free transfer. If you don't already have an IRA (you can have as many IRAs as you like), open one at a bank and put the money in a money market account until you decide where to invest long-term for your retirement.

If you keep the 401(k) or other employer plan money in a separate IRA, you could roll this IRA back into a new employer's company retirement plan at a later date. This might be a good deal if the new employer has a retirement plan you like and you feel the company can manage the money better than you can.

But these turbulent times aren't for the meek, and they're not for the average worker who squanders his or her future retirement assets changing jobs. Let's say you are changing jobs and the lump-sum distribution from your company retirement plan is $10,000. Let's also assume you have the option to roll over the money into an IRA and invest in a stock mutual fund that has an annual total return of 13 percent, or take the after-tax cash and head for the local shopping mall. If you take the cash, you'll have about $6,000 after tax to spend. If you roll it over to an IRA:

Roll It Over to IRA	Amount at Age 65
Start at age 35	$390,000
Start at age 45	115,000
Start at age 55	34,000

I've talked to a lot of people who are near retirement and they can't remember where their 401(k) rollover money went. They fully understand now that the most compelling reason for keeping the money they've already saved in a retirement plan working for them was that the $6,000 they spent on a shopping spree could have cost them as much as $400,000 when they retired!

You can only do it once!

As I frequently say on radio, "Once you've make a rollover to an IRA, you have no reverse gear." In plain English, you can't back up and start over. Therefore, before you roll money out of a qualified employer-sponsored retirement plan, remember that all the options that are available under these company plans disappear when the money lands in an IRA.

When You Get a Divorce

Money distributed from an employer's tax-qualified retirement plan under a Qualified Domestic Relations Order (QDRO) is subject to ordinary income taxes if it is not rolled over into an IRA, but is not subject to the 10 percent early withdrawal penalty even if you are under age 59½. If the money is rolled over into an IRA and later taken out to pay attorneys' fees or to buy a new car, the early withdrawal penalty could then apply. If you get a divorce and need money from a QDRO plan distribution, and you are under age 59½, it is better to use the money before you roll it over into an IRA and lose the penalty-free withdrawals.

Learn more

Company retirement plans are rapidly changing, and as I write, Congress is working on more options to allow employees to manage their own retirement accounts with possible daily or weekly changes in the assets in the plan. The Department of Labor (DOL) has proposed that employers provide full-service investment management (brokers, financial planners, money managers) for workers covered under their plans as long as there are safeguards to protect participants from self-dealing by a financial adviser.

It's also a good idea to get the free government booklet called "Your Pension: Things You Should Know About Your Pension Plan." Go to the Pension Benefit Guaranty Corporation's website, www.pbgc.gov, or call them at 202-326-4040. Another good source is "Women and Pensions: What Women Need to Know and Do." It's a free pamphlet designed to help women evaluate their pensions and plan for retirement. For a copy call the U.S. Pension and Welfare Benefits Administration at 202-219-9247 or visit their website at www.dol.gov/pwba.

Individual Retirement Accounts

Today we are faced with financial deregulation that has unleashed radical new ways to invest our money. As a result, most people are lost in a maze of advertising. Every time we pick up the newspaper or turn on the television, we see some guy offering fabulous returns on our investment dollars. The problem is, there's a lot of hoopla and not much good advice. If you open an IRA, get your hands on the facts, and stay clear of the rip-offs. This can take a substantial strain off the old fear that keeps you awake at night. In the lingo of personal finance, I want to give you the inside edge.

The most popular game ever invented is Monopoly. But its popularity was not at first apparent to the public. No one was expected to buy a crazy game where people tried to make themselves rich. But they did. Generations of Americans have bought Boardwalk and Park Place and tried to stay out of jail.

Today, a new Monopoly game is catching on. You no longer have to put hotels on Park Place, and best of all, you don't have to go to jail. The name of the game is "Finding the People's Tax Loophole."

Congress designed Individual Retirement Accounts in 1974 to tax-shelter the lesser of $1,500 or 15 percent of income each year. In designing IRAs, however, Congress was on the horns of a dilemma. The more attractive it made IRAs, the more the government would lose in tax revenues. In 1974, when Congress established the IRA program, it tried to cut the government's losses by limiting IRAs only to people who were not covered by a retirement plan where they worked. With only about 30 percent of the workforce eligible, the IRA program was plainly unfair. But the requirement that barred workers from opening an IRA if they were covered at work was misunderstood. Millions of Americans worked for companies that had retirement plans where little or, in many cases, no contributions were made on the employee's behalf. As a result, out of the estimated 30 million eligible people, only about 2.5 million (mostly higher-bracket workers) bothered to open an IRA. It turned out they could save $1,500 in an IRA and the government would pay for half their retirement costs. That kind of savings made the people's tax loophole look very attractive to high earners.

In 1982, Congress made the program even sweeter with the passage of the Economic Recovery Tax Act. The people's loophole was widened to include all working Americans, and for the first time, even part-timers could shelter part or all of their earnings. Best of all, the procedures for setting up an IRA was greatly simplified, and the opportunities to switch, diversify, and roll over your money into IRAs were expanded.

But it left a big question eating away at most Americans: Can I afford to retire? Like a detective thriller, planning our retirement income has become a mystery. What will the inflation rate be in ten or maybe twenty years when I retire? How do I save taxes and save money under the complicated IRA rules and regulations?

The good news is that planning your retirement income doesn't *have* to be a mystery. All I want you to do is cut and scrape a little each month for the money you'll need to build your IRA. I have no idea of your current income level, family responsibilities, or retirement goals. As you read this book, you'll have to dig deep into your inner soul to determine how much money you can save each year and come up with the retirement strategy that's best for you. I can't do that for you.

A Look at the Future

I'm confident that before long we'll have a new set of options to save for retirement. Here is a list of some new IRA programs that have been proposed in Congress.

Individual Housing Accounts

One idea is to allow IRA money, or money contributed to a new Individual Housing Account, to be used as part of a down payment on a principal residence. Under one bill, the money withdrawn must be used within 90 days as a down payment; for at least three years prior to withdrawal the account must be with a savings institution; and the depositor must give at least 60 days' notice before withdrawal of the funds for down payment purposes. In addition, the IHA owner must live in the house as a principal residence for at least three years. The taxes would be deferred until the home is sold. Some proposals would allow someone saving for a home to set aside up to $2,000 a year. Working couples could stash away as much as $4,000.

Mortgage Payoff Accounts

Another idea floating around Congress is to give homeowners a chance to pay off their mortgages faster than they have to. This bill would allow a deduction of $2,000 a year ($4,000 for couples) for speeding up principal payments. The sponsors claim that the tax deduction for Homeowners' IRAs to speed up mortgage payments would actually lessen government red ink. The IRA tax deduction would be far less than the interest deductions now available over the length of the mortgage.

And the beat goes on. Another new idea is for IRAs to help pay for private schooling. There's even talk of an IRA to help retrain laid-off workers for high-tech jobs. Again, no one knows when or if any of these bills may become law. But one of the best reasons to stash away your cash in an IRA may be the expanded uses that are sure to come out of Congress in the future.

Why Should You Open an IRA?

How would you like to toss away as much as $1,000 a year or more because of bum information? Surprisingly, a lot of folks are doing just that. What's sickening is that they're doing it in the area that counts most—the money they'll need to live on for the rest of their lives.

Let's assume you can cut and scrape and set aside $2,000 a year in a tax-deductible IRA and compare that with $2,000 in after-tax money. In both cases you are putting money into your piggy bank, but in only one case is the pig getting fat. Remember, this table is based on only one $2,000 deposit at the beginning of the saving period. Here's what can happen when you ignore the powerful impact taxes can have on your hard-earned dollars. The chart below measures total value of capital and accumulated interest at the end of the year with a single $2,000 investment and 12 percent annual return. Assume the return and the tax bracket remain constant during the saving period.

End of Year	Tax-Deferred IRA Account	Taxable 33% Tax Bracket
1	$2,240	$1,450
2	2,500	1,585
3	2,810	1,730
4	3,150	1,880
5	3,525	2,050
6	3,945	2,225
7	4,420	2,440
10	6,210	3,160
15	10,945	4,860

When you save for retirement, you should first save on an absolute order of priority. Until you've opened your IRA, don't worry about the stock market, that hot investment in real estate, or mutual funds. Nothing can beat the magic of making your money grow in an IRA. In fact, IRAs should be your number one piggy bank for accumulating money.

Remember, you don't have to put the annual contribution in at once. Find out how you can add to your IRA on a monthly basis so you can save the money before you spend it.

Rules of the IRA Game

Here are some of the most-asked questions about IRAs from our radio programs and from the people who write us or log onto our big web site, www.financialsavvy.com:

How much can I put into an IRA?
Up to $3,000 per person, per year, from 2002 to 2004 (or 100 percent of your pay if you earn less than the maximum), or $6,000 for a married couple. In years 2005 through 2007 the maximum contribution is $4,000, and in 2008, $5,000. After this date cost-of-living increases are scheduled to become effective in increments of $500 a year.

Workers who turn 50 and older before the end of the taxable year get to make up for lost time. From 2002 through 2005 they can contribute an extra $500, in 2006 and thereafter an extra $1,000.

But note: Your annual contributions to a regular IRA *and* a Roth IRA cannot exceed the maximum annual contribution limit. Remember, if a year goes by without a contribution, you're stuck. Under current rules you can't go back and make it up in later years.

When can I open an IRA?
Any time during the year. In fact, the sooner you open one the longer your income can grow tax-deferred. The reason you find a media blitz from January through March is that if you open an IRA and make a contribution before you file your income tax return prior to April 15, you can take a tax deduction for the previous year.

What can I put in an IRA?
You must have earned income on the job to make an IRA contribution. You can't make contributions with unearned income, such

as money you receive from investments, stock dividends, rental income, and pension payments or retirement annuities.

You can invest in gold coins made in the USA, stocks, bonds, and mutual funds and real estate, but you cannot contribute real estate in which you have a direct ownership. A nugget buried in the 1981 tax bill that expanded IRAs to all working Americans also bans investments in collectibles, such as rare coins, stamps, rugs, antiques, or fine art.

Can I transfer my IRA to another IRA?
Yes. The best way is to have the financial institution (which is acting as your custodian/trustee) send the money directly to the new financial institution. When a transfer has been made directly from one custodian/trustee to another, no taxes are due. You can make a transfer from one IRA to another as often as you like.

You can also withdraw the assets in cash. In this case you have sixty days to reinvest the money into another IRA without a tax penalty. You can make only one withdrawal and reinvestment in an IRA each year for each IRA you have.

The important point to remember is that your IRA is not glued to one financial institution forever. You have choices when you are considering an IRA, and one basic choice is deciding where to keep it. If you're not happy with your investments you can easily move your IRA from one financial institution to another. Generally, the new IRA trustee will provide transfer forms that you can sign and they will transfer the money to the new IRA.

Can I deduct IRA fees?
Yes. The money you spend to set up your IRA and for annual administrative fees, as a current cost of producing income, is deductible.

How many IRAs can I have?
As many as you want, as long as you don't exceed the maximum annual contribution each year. In most cases, you'll find you have several different rollover IRAs from employer retirement plans when you change jobs or when the employer terminates the retirement or saving plan where you work.

How can I save taxes?
You can't. All withdrawals from an IRA are taxed at the owner's state and federal ordinary tax rate, and investment losses are not tax deductible.

Can I borrow from my IRA?
You can't use your IRA as collateral for a loan or try to get around the early withdrawal penalty by borrowing from your IRA.

When can I take a tax deduction?
IRA deductible rules depend on your income and whether you are covered by an employer-sponsored retirement plan at work. But note: You are considered covered if you are covered at work for one or more days during the entire year. Here's the current schedule for allowable deductions.

If you are not covered by a retirement plan at work: Anyone who has earned income can take the full tax deduction. This applies to any income level.

If you are covered by a retirement plan at work: Now the rules get complicated.

If only one spouse is covered by a retirement plan at work, the non-working spouse can deduct an IRA contribution, but the deduction is phased out between $150,000 and $160,000 of adjustable gross income (AGI).

If an individual is an active participant in an employer-sponsored retirement plan at work, the IRA deduction is phased out depending on AGI. Here are the numbers on adjusted gross income (AGI) for 2002:

Married/filing jointly	Single
0–$54,000	0–$32,000
$64,000 and over	$44,000 and over deduction phased out

Phase-out range is increased to $40,000–$50,000 single and $60,000–$70,000 in 2003, which increases annually in $5,000 increments to 2007.

When can I take the money out?
At any time. To keep your hands out of the IRA piggy bank, however, the Internal Revenue Service may collect income tax at your ordinary rate (and state income tax if your state has the tax) and a stiff extra 10 percent tax penalty (many states also have an early withdrawal penalty) when you take out the money before you reach age 59½.

You can safely crack your IRA nest egg early, however, without the 10 percent early withdrawal penalty under age 59½ if you follow the rules under IRS section 72(t):

> You agree to make regular withdrawals based on your life expectancy. You agree to continue these withdrawals for either five years or until you reach age 59½, whichever is longer. For example, at age 58, you would have to continue payouts to age 63, a 35-year-old for 24½ years to age 59½.

There are many ways you can calculate the amount of your withdrawals. See your tax accountant or financial adviser before you consider this option. Any funds you receive from your IRA will be taxable at your ordinary tax rate.

Section 72(t) can be used to increase your income for payments of child support, alimony, mortgage payments, or for additional income to qualify for a new home loan.

You may not pay an early withdrawal penalty if:

- The withdrawal is for unreimbursed medical expenses of more than 7.5 percent of your AGI
- Payment is for medical insurance premiums after the loss of a job
- You are totally and permanently disabled
- Payments are to a beneficiary upon account owner's death
- Payments are from a long-term annuity under IRS section 72(t)
- Payouts (up to $10,000 during your lifetime) are for certain qualified first-time homebuyers
- Payments are for college tuition expenses for yourself or family members
- Withdrawals are after age 59½

When do I have to start taking out the money?

If you turned 70½ any time during the year, the deadline to begin making the required IRA withdrawals is the first working day in April the following year. If you fail to make the withdrawals, you face a 50 percent tax penalty on the amount you should have withdrawn. If not paid, this penalty accumulates and can be paid by your beneficiaries when the money is later paid out of your estate.

The required *annual withdrawals* can be made from one or more IRAs, as long as the total amount withdrawn meets the IRS guidelines. Withdrawals from an IRA are based on your remaining life expectancy. Your IRA trustee can give you the withdrawal schedule, which can also be determined by the ages of both the

IRA owner and the beneficiary. The reason for this rule is that Congress intended IRAs to be used during retirement, not as a way to save money on a tax-deferred basis for the next generation.

Until 2002, IRA owners had to make an irrevocable choice at the beginning date from four calculations to determine life expectancy, which was used to calculate how much money had to be withdrawn from this account each year. Under the new rules, most IRA owners can use one uniform life expectancy table that generally allows them to withdraw less and leave more money in their IRA for their later years or for beneficiaries. Currently, the IRS has issued a new withdrawal table the IRS Minimum Distribution Incidental Benefit Table, and this can be used as a guideline.

Age	Divisor	Age	Divisor
70	26.2	75	21.8
71	25.3	76	20.9
72	24.4	77	20.1
73	23.5	78	19.2
74	22.7	79	18.4

Divide your December 31 IRA account balance by the divisor to determine your required minimum distribution.

What happens to my IRA if I die?
You should always name a beneficiary when you open an IRA account. Named beneficiaries can then continue the IRA owner's withdrawal schedule, if any, or take out the money within five years. The new owner will pay ordinary income taxes at their rates on any money withdrawn from an IRA.

Can I give my IRA assets to a charity?
Not directly. According to the IRS, you must first withdraw the money from the IRA and pay the required taxes. Then the balance

of the money can be donated to a charity and you can take a tax deduction for the contribution.

What if I make a mistake when I make contributions to my IRA?
You can cancel an IRA or reduce your contributions prior to filing your income taxes. In this case, you won't face a penalty for early withdrawal.

Should I roll company stock over into an IRA?
If you have company stock in your plan you can save a lot of money by not rolling over the stock into an IRA. IRS (402(a)(1)) allows retirement plan participants to take distributions of company stock rather than cash or rolling over the stock into an IRA.

If you take out the shares, only the original cost of the shares is taxable at your ordinary income tax rates. Inside the IRA, future gains in the price of the stock would be taxed at your ordinary tax rate. By taking the stock out of the retirement plan, you'll pay the lower capital gains tax rate. The difference can save you thousands of dollars in taxes once you are retired.

What Is a Roth IRA?

The Roth IRA was named after Senator William Roth of Delaware, chairman of the Senate Finance Committee that approved the new plan. Roth IRAs work in the opposite direction of traditional IRAs. You do not receive a tax deduction on your contribution, but (as long as you meet certain requirements) you pay no income taxes on your withdrawal of earnings. Roth IRAs do not require withdrawals starting at age 70½, as required by regular IRAs.

Contributions

You are eligible to open a Roth IRA if you have earned income and you meet certain adjusted gross income (AGI) levels. You could be eligible to open a Roth IRA if you are single and your AGI is less than $95,000 (phased out between $95,000 and $110,000), or if you are married filing a joint return and your combined income (AGI) is less than $150,000 (phased out between $150,000 and $160,000). These levels can change with each Congress.

Withdrawals

Withdrawals of your after-tax contributions may occur at any time—tax-free and penalty-free. Earnings in your Roth IRA are not includable in income if the Roth IRA has been established for five tax years or more and you are over age 59½. The five-year holding period starts when you open the Roth, not for each contribution. Many people start a Roth IRA with a small contribution just to start the five-year clock. Then, later on, if they want to use the Roth and make withdrawals from the plan, the Roth withdrawals could be tax-free.

If you make withdrawals before the five-year holding period, and/or you are under the age of 59½, the withdrawal rules are the same as IRAs.

Education IRAs

You can make up to $2,000 in annual contributions (as of 2002) per child into an Education IRA. Eligible contributions must be in cash and made before the child reaches age 18. The contributor need not be related to the child and there is no limit to the number of individual Education IRAs a qualified contributor can set up, but all contributions for a single child are limited to the maximum in any one tax year.

To establish and make the full contributions to an Education IRA if you are single, your AGI must be less than $95,000, phased out between $95,000 and $110,000. For married couples filing jointly, the AGI must be less than $150,000, phased out between $150,000 and $160,000.

Withdrawals are excludable from your gross income to the extent that the distributions do not exceed qualified higher education expenses. They include post-secondary tuition, fees, books, supplies, equipment (computers), and certain room and board expenses. Any remaining balance must be distributed at the time the child (beneficiary) becomes 30 years old. You can transfer (roll over) the Education IRA to another child as long as the two children are in the same generation.

The 2001 tax law not only expands the types of education expenses that qualify for use with an Education IRA, it also extends the IRA's use to both public and private elementary and high schools.

College Expenses and Buying a Home

Current law lets you withdraw up to $10,000 from an IRA without an early withdrawal penalty if you're using the money to buy your first home. You can also withdraw money penalty-free to pay for college tuition for yourself, a spouse, your children, or even your grandchildren. IRA proceeds are also available penalty-free to pay for medical expenses that exceed 7.5 percent of your AGI. While these withdrawals can be penalty-free, they are not free of federal and state income taxes.

Sometimes it's difficult to bring this tax talk clearly into focus. It's not that we have trouble with the English language; it's just that the gimmicks Congress pushes us into sometimes fog over the end results. If you need more help, log onto www.ira.com.

Congratulations! You have finished this part of the book. Admittedly, this retirement stuff is heavy going. IRAs started out simple enough. However, after several major tax laws, designed to reduce the hemorrhaging flow of taxes from the newly found loopholes, the program has become confusing to most Americans.

The main point to consider: If you make a mistake with your 401(k) or IRA, you have no reverse gear.

The party is over, the deal is done. That's why is it so important to learn how these retirement plans work, because they will be a big part of your retirement income.

The sad truth is that great earnings on the job are not enough because: *What you learn today is more important than what you earn.*

And what you do with your money is more important than what it will buy today. I personally hope you have a wonderful retirement. I know you have the information to make it happen, and now it's up to you.

STEP 8

Keep the Wolf from the Door

Buy insurance for catastrophic losses, not for temporary inconvenience

Insurance protects large numbers of people from a risk that something horrible will happen—something so bad that no reasonable or responsible person would consider not having the insurance to protect themselves against the loss. While you may never collect on your insurance, the important point is that before you buy the things you want, you need to protect yourself, your family, and all that you've worked for with a guaranteed monthly income if you become disabled and can't work or if you die. These are the risks most people cannot afford to assume during their working life. On the other hand, protection against someone smashing into the trunk of your car or being abducted by aliens from a UFO is a risk you can assume.

Disability Insurance

"When you write this book," Bill Thomas told me at a seminar as he sat in his motorized wheelchair, "be sure to tell your readers what I didn't do. I spent too much money on things I didn't need and almost none on what I really needed—protection from catastrophic loss." He looked at me with deep hurt in his eyes. "I've lost my job, my home, my wife, my self-respect. Tell them that disability is a living death."

From talking to countless people like Bill, I believe disability can indeed be a *living death.* Imagine a sudden loss of income, followed by psychological depression and anxiety about what may lie ahead. You don't have to be a rocket scientist to understand that if you become disabled you would face the skyrocketing costs of medical expenses, nursing, rehabilitation, and recuperation at the same time your ability to earn an income is lost.

The odds are that three out of ten of us will be disabled for three months or more before we reach age 65. Of those, one in five will be out of work five years or more, according to the American Council of Life Insurers. And if you thought a life insurance policy was all you needed, consider this: The insurance industry says you are five times more likely to be disabled than to die during your working life. Or, consider the Consumer Federation of America and the American Council of Life Insurers survey (Associated Press, April 24, 2001). This survey found that 40 percent of the 500 workers surveyed had no long-term disability coverage and 73 percent believed they would be financially in trouble if they lost their job.

In another survey, the Life Insurance Marketing and Research Association found that only 18 percent of all workers in the United States have any long-term disability insurance. Faced with the fact that doctors today are saving the lives of more people who otherwise would have died a few years ago, millions of these uninsured individuals won't be able to go back to work for years, if ever.

Simply put, if you are the family money machine, how will your family survive if you break down?

People often think of disability insurance as something that comes with the job. However, most employers don't provide this coverage, and those that do often make it available only as an option through payroll deduction. If you have disability insurance, or before you buy a policy, it's important to understand the major factors to look for in a policy.

Waiting Period

The waiting period, sometimes called the elimination period, is the time you have to wait before the policy pays benefits. Waiting periods vary from one month to one year, but most individual policies have a 90-day period, which means you'll receive your first check about 120 days after actually becoming disabled. Long-term disability premiums are based, for the most part, on the length of the waiting period. The longer the waiting period, the lower the policy premium. A good rule of thumb is that a 90-day waiting period will reduce the premiums in half compared to a 30-day period. A 180-day waiting period can reduce the premium by half again compared to a policy with a 90-day waiting period.

Term of Benefits

Most employer group policies pay benefits for only five years, or less. Some individual policies pay benefits to age 65 for sickness, and for life in the case of an accident. The longer the insurer is on the hook to pay benefits, the more the policy will cost.

Monthly Income

The monthly benefit is based on your previous working income. Most insurers limit their risk of replacement income to around 50 to 60 percent of your regular income.

Integration

Here's something you usually don't find in self-help books. In fact, most people have no idea that long-term disability policies can have an *integration clause.* This is a fancy term for reducing the stated benefits because of other income or benefits you may receive. Insurers argue that they are only protecting you for the amount shown in the policy, and they can use other benefits you may receive to reduce their payouts.

For example, assume your regular income is $3,000 a month and your group disability policy has a $1,800-a-month benefit (60 percent of your pay). Also, assume that after you become disabled you are able to collect $500 a month from your workers' compensation plan, and $1,000 a month from Social Security after a five-month waiting period. You like the extra money, but you are thinking about your $500 off-the-rack suit revolving on your credit card and how you are going to pay your bills without a job. Then you discover what insurance sales representatives have known for years: the bottom is about to drop out of your disability income.

Concealed in the fine print of your employer group disability policy is a 50 percent integration level. If you receive $1,500 a month from other sources, as in the example above, $750 of that money could be used to reduce the insurer's monthly payout, leaving a benefit of $1,050, not $1,800 a month. While you are thinking, "They can't do that to me," consider that the money you receive from your group disability policy (to the extent the employer paid the premiums) is taxable as ordinary income.

Your Occupation

When you apply for an individual disability policy, your occupation is critical. If you are self-employed or in a high-risk business, you'll have a tough time getting coverage. If you work behind a desk in a large office building, you are in good shape. If you're just starting a business, the cost may be prohibitive.

Going Back to Work

For many employer group plans, this is the escape clause. Many of these policies will not pay benefits if you return to work, or in some cases, if you work more than a few hours a week. The trick is not to throw out your claim, but to start the waiting period over again.

How to Buy a Disability Policy

Group Employer Plans

Most disability policies today are sold as part of a group employer plan where the insurer believes a claim is unlikely. This saves the insurer money and keeps the premiums (paid for by the company and often with a contribution from the employee) as low as possible. If you leave your job, you generally lose the employer-sponsored coverage. But you can convert your supplemental plan to regular disability coverage without a medical exam. You may want to accept this offer if you can't pass a medical exam for a new individual policy.

Group policies are easy to obtain. Most employer-sponsored policies can cover people who would not otherwise qualify for an individual underwritten policy because no medical report is required to sign up. Often you just sign your name or fill out a short form and agree to pay the premiums. To keep the premiums low and allow almost any employee to sign up, these policies come loaded with fine print and ways the insurer can avoid paying claims or reduce the benefits. Only when a claim is filed with the carrier begin the underwriting process and determine if the claim can or must be paid.

Level Premiums

Many insurance policies for disability, health care, nursing home, or other risks often promise that the premiums will not increase due to your age or physical condition. That sounds like a level premium policy, doesn't it? The problem is a common boilerplate disclaimer that says future premiums may rise. It turns out that the promise the insurers made not to raise premiums on *your individual policy* does not exclude their right to raise premiums for the *entire group* of which you are a part. In other words, if your group (generally understood to include those who bought similar policies) as a whole ages and starts filing an increased number of claims, the insurer might simply raise the premiums for all policyholders in the group.

Individual Policies

These policies are fully underwritten from the start. You probably will be asked to take a medical exam, provide your medical history, give evidence of your income, and agree to let the insurer take a peek at your driving record and other personal history. As you get older, these policies can become difficult to buy because the insurer can be locking in a guarantee to pay out a sum that could exceed a life insurance contract. For example, say you are age 45 and buy a $2,000-a-month policy payable to age 65 for sickness and for life in the event of an accident. If the claims were to start in the first year, the carrier could be on the hook for almost half a million dollars!

Individual disability policies usually can't be canceled, except for non-payment of premium. Like whole life insurance, once the policy is issued premiums usually remain the same for the life of the policy. Because disability underwriting standards are the toughest in the insurance industry, and because your health is a paramount issue, the best time to buy a long-term disability policy is when you are under 45 and in good health.

Life Insurance

My good friend Paul rode his bicycle to work each day. He said it was good exercise, and besides, he saved a half hour on his commute by taking the back roads off the highway. One day I got a call. A truck suddenly came out of a driveway and Paul could not avoid a head-on collision. Four hours later, he died in the hospital. I'll never forget the look on his widow's face when she found out that Paul had only $25,000 of group life insurance, not even enough to pay the hospital and funeral bills.

With two young children to raise, she told me she had no idea how she could pay the bills and continue to live in their home. What makes this message about life insurance so painful for me is what I could not tell his wife: Paul could have applied for and put in force a $250,000 life insurance policy for less than twenty dollars a month!

Don't skimp on your life insurance protection.

Many authors can tell you how to get rich in America today, but no one can tell your family or loved ones how to survive in the event you aren't there to make your millions in the market. Life insurance can do that.

The idea of life insurance is quite simple: If 10,000 people chip in $10 each and one person dies during the year, the death benefit could be $100,000. No one knows, of course, who will die during the year but, with a $10 bill, you have eliminated a risk at a very low cost. Obviously for an insurer to be able to pay out benefits to all the policyholders who die every year, they need to insure a great many more people.

Life insurance is the business of taking a risk on death.

Since life insurance death benefits were likely to be paid to widows and orphans who needed every dollar they could collect, Congress long ago gave the benefits special tax treatment: they are received income-tax-free by the beneficiaries. The premium payments, however, are normally—but not always—made with after-taxable income.

Life Insurance Premium Classes

- **Preferred Best** If you can run a five-minute mile on the beach or you're as healthy as Superman, you may qualify for the lowest cost life insurance. As you might guess, most insurance companies advertise with rates for preferred best clients. To qualify, you must not have a history of health impairments, a high-risk occupation or avocations, or take prescription medication. You must have an acceptable height-to-weight ratio and an absence of immediate family history risk factors, such as heart disease or cancer.
- **Preferred** This definition is less stringent than for Preferred Best. You may take certain prescription medication, weigh a bit more, or have limited family history of risk factors.
- **Standard** If you can't qualify for either of the above because of personal or family history, you may still qualify as Standard.
- **Tobacco Use** Tobacco use will shoot your premiums skyward like a rocket. Most issuers will not issue Preferred Best or Preferred if you smoke. Others allow some exceptions for cigars, pipes, or nicotine gum or patches. Some companies may consider you a nonsmoker if you have quit the use of cigarettes for longer than one year. Other companies consider you a smoker

until your last cigarette is at least two, three, or even five years behind you.

If you smoke, your classification could be standard smoker, and typically your premiums will be more than double the regular standard rate.

Waiver of Premium Rider

This rider will pay the annual premiums if you are disabled and can't work. This low-cost rider is a good idea because if you allow the policy to lapse from nonpayment of premiums when you are disabled, your health may not allow you to buy new life insurance in the future.

The next step is to look at the various kinds of policies.

Whole Life Insurance

The most frequently asked question about life insurance is: Should I buy term or whole life? A recent study conducted by the Guardian Insurance Company found that a whole life policy was a better overall long-term buy if you kept it in force at least ten years. That said, very few policyholders keep their policies in force that long. In fact, according to insurance company records, *only 3 percent of policyholders keep their permanent policies in force for twenty years.*

What the study did not address is that a 35-year-old male with a growing family would prioritize death protection and lower annual premiums over long-term savings for retirement. While the whole life annual premium for the $250,000 policy is $2,900, the twenty-year level premium term coverage for the same account for a nonsmoker is only about $200 a year. Since these premiums come from after-tax dollars, and your federal income tax bracket is likely to be 28 percent, the percentage of your salary these premiums represent is even greater.

Disappearing Cash Values

The cash value buildup in your policy, often illustrated with glowing numbers that promise wealth at retirement, can be an illusion. In the event of the policyholder's death, the insurance company first pays off any policy loans. The fine print reads: "The amount of your outstanding loan, and unpaid interest charges if any, will be deducted from the death benefit that is payable to the beneficiary." Say, for example, that upon your death you hold a $100,000 whole life policy from which you borrowed $30,000; the insurer will pay only $70,000 to your beneficiaries and cancel the outstanding loan.

The even worse news is that you've haven't heard all the bad news. In the event of your death, the company will also take the cash values to help pay the death benefit. If you have a $100,000 life policy with a $45,000 cash-value balance, it will cost the insurer only $55,000 to pay the death benefit. You have, in effect, already paid for a large part of the money that will be paid to your beneficiaries.

The bottom line is that the cash values don't belong to you.

Whole life polices are usually sold based on the illustrations of future cash values that spin out of the insurer's computers. These are, for the most part, based on guesswork. To make the policies more attractive, the illustrations are frequently based on various interest rate assumptions and mortality rates, often higher than those actually used by the insurer. The bottom line is this: The cash-value build-up shown in the computer-generated illustrations is not a guarantee, and sometimes not even a good guess, of how the policy is going to look in 20 years or when you reach age 65.

How do the insurance companies get away with dangling the promise of future riches before prospective policy buyers? A look at the fine print will reveal something like this: "This is an illustration, not a contract." You can take advantage of the cash value of the policy in other ways: You can borrow some of the cash values and pay current interest rates on the loan; use the cash value to buy a paid-up whole life policy with a smaller death benefit; or withdraw your money and cancel the policy. If you withdraw the cash values, you will pay ordinary income taxes on any buildup over the years, just as you would from a tax-deferred annuity.

Term Life Insurance

A term policy is similar to auto and fire insurance. Your annual premium covers only one year of protection. A term policy typically has no cash value and pays no dividends. Term life is sold with level premiums for one year (Annual Renewable Term), five, ten, twenty, and even twenty-five years. At the end of these periods, the insurance is renewable at higher premiums based on the policyholder's age and health.

Another form of term insurance is *decreasing term,* in which the annual premium remains the same but the death benefit declines. These term policies are usually sold to pay off a mortgage on the theory that, while the death benefit declines each year, so does the balance on mortgage.

Invest or Rent?

When you buy life insurance, you have two basic choices: "Invest" in a whole life policy with savings for retirement, or "rent" term insurance protection with much lower premiums.

If the annual premium for a $250,000 whole life policy for a 35-year-old non-smoking male is about $2,900, while a 20-year level-premium term policy is about $200, that's an annual savings of $2,700. Over twenty years that's $54,000. If you invested the savings from buying the term policy each year in a good stock fund returning the historical average of about 13 percent a year, you could have about $246,000 in your investment account when your twenty-year term policy expires. At age 55 you would become your own life insurance company.

The disadvantage with term life insurance is that after the level premiums in the policy expire, you may need to medically requalify for a policy and pay higher premiums. In the case of the 35-year-old with a $250,000 policy, the annual premiums of $200 for the first twenty years could jump to about $400 at age 45, and to about $900 at age 55. On the other hand, if he or she runs their "own" life insurance company, they have the money to pay the higher premiums or self-insure.

Internet Insurance Shopping

Companies that specialize in finding the cheapest term life insurance began to appear in the late 1980s. They all share three common features.

First, one brief contact may help you find some real bargains in term life insurance. That's because term insurance is a one-price product that lends itself to computerized comparisons. A twenty-year level premium term plan from the same insurance company should have the same rates in San Francisco or Chicago.

Second, an agent does not visit. All activity is via the Internet, phone, fax, and/or mail.

Third, most shopping services will help you purchase the life insurance they quote. In all instances, their compensation comes from the insurance company after you have accepted the insurance by paying the premium. Most insurers now require a medical exam, paid for by the insurance company, for amounts over $100,000.

One important feature to check is the guarantee of level premiums. For example, in a twenty-year level-premium plan, rates may be guaranteed for only the first five years and estimated thereafter with a much higher guaranteed premium stated in the policy. These *mixed-rate plans* allow the insurer to limit its liability after the initial five-year premium period. Some insurers, however, will guarantee the full ten or twenty years without the mixed rates.

In all states, you get a twenty- or thirty-day "free" look at a new insurance policy. During this period, you can examine and return the policy for any reason without obligation. You can even receive a refund on any premium paid.

Lower Premiums Today

Fortunately for the consumer, competition among insurance companies has driven annual premiums down in the past six to eight years to historic lows. If you shop wisely today you can save as much as 30 to 60 percent on new life insurance.

Here are some points to consider:

- If your term life policy is more than three years old and your current health is good, you could save serious money with a good shopping service.
- More costs relatively less. There is little competition in term life plans of less than $100,000. But starting at $100,000, you can substantially reduce your premium cost per thousand dollars of benefit.
- Watch for breakpoints. These set the limits for reductions in the cost per thousand of death benefits. These typically occur at

$100,000, $150,000, $250,000 and, with some companies, at $500,000.

- Always select companies with superior or excellent financial ratings. Top ratings from at least two of the five major rating services make for good "sleep insurance."
- Always remember the most important factor in your premiums is your health definition. The Preferred Best premiums can be at least 50 percent lower than those of a standard smoker's policy.

Variable Life

Because term insurance premiums are so inexpensive and whole life insurance pays such low rates of return, insurers now offer other policies, such as universal life and variable life, which allow insureds to invest in mutual funds and other securities with higher rates of return. Think of these policies as a cross between a variable annuity and a life insurance policy. The policyholder can let the assets grow tax-deferred until the money is withdrawn or passed on tax-free to the beneficiary as life insurance death benefits.

One of the selling points is that if you pay large premiums for a limited number of years—and your mutual funds perform well—the policy can become fully funded. That is, the investments generate enough income to cover the insurance premiums and fees. The problem is that the length of time for a policy to become fully funded is based on *estimated* mutual fund performance when the policy is sold. If the fund's total returns are lower than estimated, you can end up paying premiums far longer than you originally expected. If you need to borrow money from the policy at current interest rates, you must withdraw a matching amount from the policy's underlying equity mutual funds and put it into a money market account as collateral. As a result, policy loans are not encouraged because they limit the ability of the underlying investments to earn enough to cover the policy's fees and annual insurance costs.

However, to get this annuity in a life insurance wrapper, the policyholder pays hefty fees and assumes several risks. In fact, these fees can be so mind-boggling that most people—agents and consumers—don't understand precisely how much they cost the policyholder. They often come with high expense ratios to keep the policy in force, high costs of buying and selling the funds, and high annual management fees. In addition, *surrender penalties* can run to half the money you originally invested. The termination charges usually decline over the first five or ten years the policy is in force. Many experts estimate that it can take from ten to 20 years for you to break even after the fees, depending on how much you pay into the policy each year and how the mutual funds you've selected perform.

Typically, for a nonsmoking male age 35 with a $250,000 variable universal life policy and an average annual gain of 10 percent, the premiums paid and the account value after the first five years are just about even. After ten years, such a person's annual return is about 6 percent, and after twenty years, about 9 percent. As a result, variable life policies can also be the most expensive type of life insurance you can buy.

What Are Your Options?

You could combine term life insurance with a Standard & Poor's 500 stock index mutual fund and cut your monthly outlay by more than half. If you do, you will:

- Lose your tax-deferral on the asset buildup inside a whole life policy. But since index stock funds are rarely traded, most of your capital gains will come when you make withdrawals. Then you'll pay lower capital gains tax rates instead of ordinary rates as you would on withdrawals from a variable life insurance policy.

- Leave more to your beneficiary. They will receive not only the face value of the term life insurance policy, but the entire mutual fund buildup. With a variable or whole life policy, the insurance company keeps the cash values to pay part of the death benefit.

Second-to-Die Policies

The increasingly popular second-to-die policy pays the death benefit on the death of the last spouse. Its premiums are substantially less than separate policies for the same total amount. The purpose of such a policy is to provide the life insurance proceeds to pay the estate taxes on the second death. You can take out new policies, but exchanges of a couple's separate life policies for a joint second-to-die policy will not qualify for tax-free exchanges, and any gains that have accrued in the original policies would be taxable income.

Accelerated Death Benefits

You might want to take advantage of the latest wrinkle in the life insurance industry, an accelerated death benefit (ADB) rider. With a growing number of people diagnosed with AIDS and cancer, more than 150 life insurers now allow policyholders to collect all or part of the death benefit early if they are terminally ill with less than twelve months to live. A recent IRS ruling gives these early payouts the same tax treatment as regular death benefits.

How to Learn More

National Insurance Consumer Association

The group is sponsored by the insurance industry and has a help line (800-942-4242) where specialists will answer your questions and send you information on all aspects of disability and life insurance.

Medical Information Bureau

Ever wonder how the insurance companies learn about your risk of dying from a heart attack, how often you skydive, your driving habits, and other personal information? It's easy. It takes about two minutes for the insurer to plug into the insurance industry's huge data bank at the Medical Information Bureau (MIB) near Boston. Most of the American and Canadian insurers use this database to help them underwrite your application for a health, life, or disability policy.

The MIB's records may be updated every time you apply for insurance. A report is sent if the underwriter believes that the applicant's medical or background check indicates a higher-than-average risk or the potential for fraud. Because this watchdog group is watching over each application, it's a good idea to be completely honest about your medical and personal history when you apply for insurance.

To learn more about the MIB, go to their website at www.mib.com or write for their free booklet, "The Consumer's MIB Fact Sheet," and for instructions on how to request a copy of your personal file (MIB, Box 105, Essex Station, Boston, MA 02112; in Canada, MIB, 330 University Avenue, Toronto, Canada M5G 1R7).

STEP 9

Someone to Help You

Do your homework before you use a financial planner.

Say your financial plans are a mess. You thought your nest egg was on bedrock, but it's crumbling. You may be thinking about turning to a financial planner or broker for help. After all, you tell yourself, they're the pros in the money business, right? We're not talking about some no-name broker from an unknown firm who makes a lot of money dumping your hard-earned cash into some disastrous investment, but a real pro.

I did my basic financial planning over a hay rake in my dad's farm machine shop, where I learned that financial planning included managing my monthly paycheck so I had something left over each month to invest. I learned not to put too much money into my house so I could put more into the asset column, which I did even in my early years. I also kept something in reserve for when things went wrong. My dad taught me that growing up dirt poor was not as good as growing up rich and living in a family that actually owned a car and more than two changes of clothes per person. While I made all my plans on my own, things have gotten considerably more complicated since then, and you may feel you need a financial adviser to help you start building your retirement nest egg.

To those who feel a professional's advice will help them sleep better, a word of warning: The Consumer Federation of America reports that the financial planning business is a potential minefield for unwary consumers. At the heart of the problem is the fact that anyone who can hang a sign and pay to have cards printed can claim to be a financial planner. So it's no wonder there are somewhere between 200,000 and 300,000 people in the United States who call themselves financial planners.

Originally, financial planning and money management services were aimed primarily at the wealthy, and the industry was based on "single-product" sales. Life insurance agents sold life insurance, brokers bought and sold stocks and bonds, and banks offered savings accounts. But with financial firms invading each other's turf, insurance agents, brokers, and bankers all call themselves one-stop financial planners, though few started out that way. They often push investors toward the in-house investments or the products they know best, which may or may not be in the client's best interest.

The truth is, in the business of mass marketing, many salespeople are load-driven. The first-year commission for a whole life policy can run as much as 60 percent or more of the initial premium, an annuity of from 5 to 6 percent. Because of these large commissions, the surrender cash value for the life policy can be zero after the first year and only 35 percent after the second year. An annuity might have a surrender charge of around 6 to 8 percent of the assets withdrawn within the first few years.

Before you seek a financial planner or broker, consider this: Unless you have at least $100,000 outside your 401(k) or other company-sponsored tax-qualified retirement plans, or you regularly invest in common stocks, bonds, or have a brokerage account, you probably don't have enough money to attract a planner to manage your assets. In some large brokerages, the money manager earns only 0.6 percent of the money he has under management. For an account to be profitable, the investment should be at least $250,000.

The worst mistake you can make, and it could cost you a fortune, is to turn over your money to a financial planner without first understanding how the money will be invested and what it will cost you to use his or her services. Also, before you trust someone to handle your money, find out all you can about his or her personal and professional reputation for integrity and competence. After all, you wouldn't allow a stranger to drive your car. Why would you let one handle your money?

How to Select a Planner

Getting a handle on a good financial planner today is a lot like trying to roller-skate in a room filled with marbles. Not only must you navigate a maze of investment products and decipher industry jargon (and often overly optimistic projections of what you'll earn), but you must also be sure the investments you do make will let you sleep at night. Before you select a financial planner, here are some things you should investigate.

Payment for Services

When you take your television set or car to be repaired, you get an estimate before the work is undertaken, but the cost of a financial planner's services are often vague and they will depend on how the planner is paid.

Commission-Only

Under this arrangement, you pay no fees for the planner's services. He or she is compensated by sales commissions from life insurance, annuities, mutual funds, partnerships, or other investments you purchase. A conflict of interest can exist when the planner depends entirely on commission income. Often, the riskier the investment, the richer the commissions, and the greater the incentive for the planner to suggest that you include them in your portfolio. There is nothing wrong with buying these products, but you should be aware that commission income could differ, depending on the type of product. Planners can also often receive trailer commissions, which are paid every quarter or year on the total assets in your account. If you select a commission-only planner, it's a good idea to ask for a written statement of how much he or she will earn for each type of product, and it's best to get this information before you buy anything through them.

Fee-Based

Fee-based, or fee-plus-commission planners, often charge a flat fee for advice and for working up a financial plan. They typically earn a commission on any products they sell implementing the plan, and they can receive annual fees for managing the assets. Once you have paid the planner's fee, however, you have no obligation to buy any products, but many planners will reduce their fees if you do.

Fee-Only

These planners work much like an accountant or lawyer, charging only for their time at a typical rate of around $200 an hour. The initial fee to produce a financial plan can run anywhere from $500 to $5,000 or more, depending on the planner, your assets, and your age. Although fee-only planners won't sell you financial products, they are often helpful in finding no-load or low-load investments, and they are free to suggest any financial investment. Before you select a fee-only planner, be sure to set limits on his or her hourly fees for the work you want done. Many fee-only planners can also provide a program to monitor your investments, usually for a charge of around 1 to 2 percent a year of the assets under management.

Annual-Fee

This is the fastest-growing segment of the financial planning business. Typically, you'll pay a $200 to $500 fee for a personal financial plan. The advisor then works with you to determine your risk tolerance and designs an investment portfolio. You can also receive quarterly statements of your account for an annual fee of 1.5 percent to 2 percent or more, based on the total assets under management.

In-House Planner

Many banks, savings and loans, and other organizations offer financial planning services. In most instances, financial planners on their staff earn a salary and commissions. They can also earn bonuses for sales performance. The financial institution is compensated directly by the mutual fund or other financial products or services. You are, however, often limited to the investment products that are available from that financial institution.

Educational Level

You should be aware that some financial planners are little more than single-product salespeople with little or no government or industry supervision. Others are professionals who face industry, state, and federal government regulators. Some have little formal education, while others have a bachelor's or master's degree with professional designations. Unfortunately, federal regulators such as the Securities and Exchange Commission keep track of only a handful of planners. Many other people who purport to be financial planners report their activities to almost no one.

The initials after a planner's name do not guarantee competence or ethics, but they often indicate that the person has been in business for at least three years and has made the effort to learn his or her trade by completing a two-year college-level course. The most popular professional designation is Certified Financial Planner (CFP). To become a CFP, a planner must pass a two-day, college-level exam and agree to follow a code of ethics. CFP holders must also complete thirty hours of continuing education every two years to retain the designation. CFPs, like holders of other financial-planning professional designations, are not licensed or certified by any state agency.

The Chartered Financial Consultant (ChFC) designation for financial planners and the Chartered Life Underwriter (CLU) designation for professional life insurance agents are both given by the Society of Financial Service Professionals. To maintain high standards, the members must complete sixty hours of continuing education every two years. Many planners hold the CFP and the ChFC designations, and many also hold the CLU designation.

A financial planner may also be a Registered Investment Adviser under the Investment Advisers Act of 1940, and registered with the Securities and Exchange Commission (SEC). A Registered Investment Adviser is required to keep detailed records and books and to follow specific guidelines for advertising and claims made to clients or prospective clients.

You can discount the fancy material you may receive from a planner. When you interview a professional SEC Registered Investment Adviser, you want to focus on two documents. The first is the disclosure statement, which must be given to a prospective client before any work begins. Among other things, the disclosure statement outlines the planner's services and fees, types of clients, education, background, and other business activities. The second document is Part II of your planner's ADV form, which must be filed with the SEC and often the state. Sign each copy and retain one for your files.

Possible Conflicts of Interest

Many planners work under contract to sell their firm's mutual funds and other products. You may not realize that many of the in-house products carry a higher commission than those offered by independent investment firms. In some cases, your investment could be a ticket to the next convention in Florida for the planner and his or her spouse. Most planners will tell you that they can recommend the best investment for you from any source, and many can, but it's a good idea to find out just how many financial products the planner regularly offers to clients. Hiring a planner who represents several financial firms does not guarantee that you'll make more money than you would with one who offers only one company's products. However, one of the things you are paying for is the planner's independent judgment, and that often involves surveying the entire field to find the best products for your individual situation.

Background

It's a good idea to find out whether the planner has ever been the subject of disciplinary action by any federal or state agency or professional body, or been involved in arbitration proceedings with former clients. Any experienced planner will have worked with hundreds of clients and will have lost money for some of them. The investment business, with or without a planner's help, does not always produce big gains. Some clients don't fully understand the risks; others expect their investments to skyrocket. When their investments turn sour, the planner is bound to get some complaints. Nevertheless, some planners have a list of complaints that goes well beyond the routine.

You can contact the National Association of Securities Dealers (NASD) to find out if a planner has been the subject of any disciplinary proceedings during the past three years by the SEC or NASD or of any criminal indictments by the U.S. Department of Justice. If the planner has had problems, the NASD will mail you the information. Contact NASD, Public Disclosure Program, Box 9401, Gaithersburg, MD 20898–9401; 800-289-9999. You can also log onto www.nasd.org.

You can also call the North American Securities Administration Association (NASAA) at 202-737-0900 for the number of your state's securities department, or log onto www.nasaa.org. Your state regulator can enter the name of an individual or firm into a nationwide computer database maintained jointly by the NASAA and the NASD. The program, Central Registration Depository (CRD), tracks the person's education and employment history and indicates whether he or she has ever been the subject of a complaint or filed for bankruptcy.

On the web you can log onto www.sec.gov and check out Brokers and Advisers, the complaint center, and the U. S. Securities and Exchange Commission's activities.

Interview the Planner

After you have selected several financial planners for consideration, make an appointment to visit them in their offices. The initial visit normally is without charge. Here is where you learn if you can work with the planner and find out whether or not you feel comfortable with the process. I suggest you pose a problem on how to invest some of your money. If the answer is in line with your comfort zone, you know you have a planner who thinks like you do. If the answer fills you with scary visions of financial ruin, you know you're in the wrong office.

It's a good idea to ask for the names of current clients with whom the planner has worked, but be careful that these names are not special clients who are sure to give a favorable report. Ask for a copy of financial plans that were tailored for clients with circumstances similar to your own. In the records, you can see whether the planner followed up and how skillfully he stayed on top of the client's lifestyle and financial changes.

Monitoring Your Financial Planner

If you already have a financial planner or broker, you typically have invested in ten, twenty, or even thirty different securities. When you get your statements of accounts you may not see *how much you originally paid for the security.* This figure is important if you want to compare the current value on the statement with your cost to determine your total return. Keep the original cost information handy and make the comparisons between cost and current market value each time you receive a statement.

The chances are you will also not find the *individual or portfolio total returns for the past year, and the past three and five years.* These are numbers that will tell you how you are doing with each investment and your overall portfolio. As a result, many people have dozens of individual investments, but they don't know the annual total return for each investment, nor the total annual return for the assets managed by the broker or financial planner.

Never take a recommendation you don't fully understand.

Another pitfall to avoid is investing in something that is not suitable to your risk level or age. If you establish a relationship with a planner and receive recommendations to invest in real estate, energy, commodities, partnerships, or non-liquid long-term investments, take the time to consult a third party, such as a CPA or attorney, to determine the level of risk and whether the investment is appropriate for you. We often receive letters and calls from radio listeners who have plunked down tens of thousands of dollars in supposed high-yielding long-term investments that have gone sour. The cost of a few hundred dollars to run the proposal by an independent adviser first would have been the best investment they could have made to keep their nest eggs intact.

Remember, never make an investment decision in a hurry. If a planner or broker says it's a hot deal and they are almost out, pass. Often such planners are "load pushers" hoping the investor will listen to their pitch, rather than try to understand the possible pitfalls and risks. Pass again.

Here's one of many letters I've received from investors seeking safety and tempted by these promised higher returns. The letter is from a 66-year-old lady who invested in long-term and non-liquid limited partnerships.

"At that time, I told the broker I only wanted to invest in something very conservative since this was money I saved all my working life," she said. "I told him I did not want to lose it. I needed this money for my retirement. He suggested the partnerships, and told me it was almost guaranteed so I could feel safe about it. The rest is history. Whenever I call him, he just says to hold on. I did, and now they are worth very little."

Another trick used by some commission-hungry brokers and

planners is to encourage you to move from one mutual fund group to another. Before you do, find out whether the move is appropriate for you, whether you can afford to pay the taxes on any gains on investments held outside a tax-qualified retirement plan, and whether the sale of the funds you already own is to raise money to purchase funds with a new front-end load.

How to Find a Financial Planner

Referrals

Many people think they need a referral from a trusted adviser or friend in order to find a good financial planner. Word of mouth from someone you trust can be a good way to find a financial planner, but the person making the referral may know little or nothing about what the planner actually does. You might also get a name from someone whom the individual has known on a social rather than a professional level. And there is always the chance that the person making the referral is being paid to pass along your name. For many people who don't work directly in the financial planning field, this is a good source of income. Use referrals as a starting point and visit the planner, but do your homework before you agree to work with someone.

Professional Organizations

The following organizations can be an excellent sources for finding a good financial planner. They can provide you with the names of good financial planners in your area who meet all of the professional qualifications and have a well-established business. When you call the local planner, ask for a free first-time meeting and fact-finding session.

The Financial Planning Association (FPA). One of the best places to start is the FPA. As of January 1, 2000, the International

Association of Financial Planning (IAFP) formed the FPA. Since 1985, this organization has been a leader in establishing regulations for financial planners. Its members are expected to adhere to professional standards of ethics and practices. This group will send names and biographies of three of its top planners in your area, along with brochures titled *How a Financial Planner Can Help You,* and *How to Choose the Right One,* which includes 12 key questions to ask a planner. The organization also maintains a list of the top planners in the nation, those who have met the highest standards in the industry for experience, education, and practical knowledge. For more information, contact the FPA, 5775 Glendridge Dr. NW, Suite B-300, Atlanta, GA 30328, call 1-800-282-7526, or go online at www.fpanet.org.

The Society of Financial Service Professionals (SFSP) awards the CLU and ChFC professional designations. They will send you a list of up to five professional planners in your area and a free consumer booklet, *How to Pick a Good Professional Planner.* Contact SFSP, 270 S. Bryn Mawr Ave., Bryn Mawr, PA 19010, call 1-888-243-2258 or go online at www.financialpro.org.

The National Association of Personal Financial Advisors (NAPFA). This is a nonprofit organization that advances the practice of fee-only financial planning. In order to belong to NAPFA, a financial planner may not receive any economic benefit when a client implements his or her recommendations, including (but not limited to) commissions, rebates, awards, finder's fees, and bonuses. Members must also have either a CFP, ChFC, or CPA professional designation and must complete thirty hours of continuing professional education each year. For a list of fee-only planners in your area and a free booklet, "Why You Should Select a Fee-Only Advisor," contact NAPFA, 1130 Lake Cook Rd., Suite 105, Buffalo Grove, IL 60089, call 1-888-333-6659, or go online at www.napfa.org.

You're On Your Own, Baby

Time magazine's cover on January 28, 2002, told us "So many choices and no one to trust. In today's world you're on your own, baby." Make no mistake about it, the average investor was let down over the past two years of plunging technology and dot-com stocks, Enron disasters, and IPOs, and the results are that often 50, 60, or even 70 percent of their financial assets have disappeared in a cloud of smoke.

The lesson from all of this is that if you invest in mutual funds, stocks, or other securities *you must take the time to look after your own portfolio.* It's unlikely Fidelity or Vanguard is going to call you and say, "By the way, the mutual fund you invested in is going down the tank." For most investors it's also unlikely that the broker or planner who sold them the "can't-miss investment" is going to call and say, "Boy, did I make a mistake. We've got to sell this turkey right away." As *Time* magazine says, you're on your own.

The bottom line is that nothing is more important in investing than to admit that you made a mistake. But inertia is a strong force. For many people the inclination to leave one's investments alone usually trumps any urge to make a change. As the stocks or fund declined, many investors used the argument that "There's no point in selling now, because I've already lost so much. How much worse can it get?" As we all know after 2000 and 2001, it can get a lot worse. Big-name stocks have fallen from around $80 a share to a dollar a share and many of the original investors are still hanging on for a turnaround.

The other argument is that investors don't want to give up the hope of making money on their investment, or perhaps they want to get even before they get out. But a loss of 50 percent takes a 100 percent gain to break even. Even if that is possible, how long will it take? Five years? Ten years? Maybe never. What could you have made on your investments over this period if you hadn't lost the money?

There is also a psychological cost to hanging on to stocks or funds that have lost a big chunk of your nest egg. You can be distracted from focusing on the better investments you need to make to stem your losses and rebuild your capital base.

The Ten-Minute Rule

If you own mutual funds and/or stocks you need to understand that this ownership carries the responsibility of managing your own portfolio. Thousands of investors have called me on the radio, e-mailed me, or written telling me they have lost 50 percent or more of their retirement account and they want to know what to do.

My advice to them and to you is to spend ten minutes each Saturday with a copy of the business section of *The New York Times* and check each of your holdings over the past week. If a fund or stock has fallen more than 10 percent from its purchase price or recent high, *sell.* Don't ask questions, don't call anyone, *sell.* Every broker, discount broker, or money manager has a cash account where you can sit on the sidelines until the stock or fund comes back—if it does.

The next defensive thing you can do if you have stocks traded on the exchange is place a stop loss order (mutual funds do not allow stop loss orders) with your broker. Say your stock is currently selling for $50 a share and you don't keep your eyes glued to CNBC or the market every day. You could place a stop loss order to sell whenever the stock trades at $45 a share (the difference between the current market price and the stop loss price depends on the stock and its past trading pattern). If the stock falls to $45, the stop loss order becomes a market order and your stock is immediately sold.

The risk is that the stock could fall to $45, your order is executed, and then in a major turnaround the stock could soar to $60 a share. You would have been "stopped out" at $45 and no longer own the stock. But that's a small risk when, like millions of other investors, you could hold a $50 stock selling for $6 a share.

The old saying on Wall Street now comes into better focus:

Most investors lose more money when stocks go down than they make when they go up.

I don't know if you need a financial planner or not. After reading this book, you may decide you can start your own financial plan and build your nest egg up to a point where it makes sense to engage a planner or financial adviser, or sit down with a planner or broker and see what they recommend to build your assets over the years.

The important point is that choosing a financial planner is similar to choosing any professional in whom you place a great deal of faith. If you feel things aren't working out right, don't hesitate to switch planners. After all, no one else is going to feel the pain in your stomach when you discover the bottom has dropped out of your retirement nest egg.

GLOSSARY

adjustable-rate mortgage (ARM) A mortgage in which the interest rate is adjusted according to an index semiannually or annually to reflect changes in interest rates.

after-tax income Income on which you've paid taxes. After-tax contributions to a retirement plan or annuity can be returned tax-free, but the earnings are taxable when withdrawn.

aggressive growth fund A mutual fund that seeks maximum capital growth through investments that involve greater-than-ordinary risk, such as borrowing money, using leverage, short-selling, and options.

American depositary receipts (ADRs) Certificates of ownership in foreign stocks that are held by American banks. The bank then issues receipts for these shares, which then trade on U.S. stock exchanges or in the over-the-counter market.

American Stock Exchange The second largest stock exchange after the New York Stock Exchange; based in New York City.

amortization The gradual repayment of a debt by a series of periodic payments. Each payment includes interest and part of the principal. A mortgage is amortized over the life of the loan.

annual percentage rate (APR) The cost of borrowing money, such as a home equity or car loan, expressed as an annual percentage.

annual percentage yield (APY) APY is the total interest your account will earn at the end of one year. A balance of $1,000 with an APY of 5 percent will total $1,050 at the end of one year.

annuity An insurance contract that allows either frequent or single contributions invested either in the stock market (variable annuity) or in a savings account (fixed annuity), and that pays a guaranteed rate of return. Payouts can start immediately after purchase (immediate annuity) or at some future date (deferred annuity). Most annuities allow the income to build up tax-deferred, like an IRA, until the money is withdrawn.

asset allocation fund A mutual fund in which portfolio managers make the allocation between cash, bonds, and stocks and buy and sell each asset as they believe market conditions warrant.

automatic reinvestment plan The process by which a mutual fund allows investors to automatically use their dividends and capital gains distributions to buy more shares. This allows a more rapid buildup of assets through the effects of compounding.

automatic withdrawal plan A plan whereby a mutual fund allows investors to receive a fixed amount of money, usually each month or quarter. For retirees, it's a way to make withdrawals for income and yet keep the bulk of the assets working in the mutual fund.

average annual yield The return on your savings over one year. A five-year CD may pay five percent a year, but with compounding of interest income, the average annual yield over the term of the CD might exceed six percent.

average daily balance (ADB) Used by banks and credit card issuers to calculate the average amount in the account. For banks, the ADB is often used to figure bank charges. For credit cards it's used to figure interest costs on credit balances.

back-end load A sales commission paid when you sell a mutual fund or annuity, not when you buy. Also known as redemption fees. These fees may be "downgraded" each year you hold the asset. For example, a 6 percent redemption fee might decline one percent each year until the sixth year, when the fee would be eliminated.

balanced fund A mutual fund in which portfolio managers "balance" the fund's assets between cash, bonds, and stocks. Considered one of the most conservative funds, it allows fund managers to spread their risk as market conditions warrant.

basis point A unit that measures the change in interest rates and bond yields. One basis point equals .01 percent of yield. An increase of 2 percent would be a change of 200 basis points.

bearer bond A bond certificate held by the owner with coupons to collect interest due. Little-used today, bearer bonds are not registered in the name of the owner by the issuer but are owned by the person holding the certificates. Bonds issued today are in registered form.

bear market A market in which prices are declining or are expected to decline.

before-tax return The return before all taxes have been paid.

beneficiary The person named to receive the benefits of an insurance policy or other asset after the death of the owner.

bid and ask price The bid price is the highest price a buyer is willing to pay; the ask price is the lowest price at which a security is offered for sale. Used in the over-the-counter market.

big board Generally another name for the New York Stock Exchange.

blue chip A term used to describe stocks and bonds issued by large, nationally known corporations.

bond A security that represents debt of the issuing entity. The issuer is usually required to pay a specific rate of interest at set times and then repay the principal upon maturity.

bond basic risk The risk in holding bonds when interest rates change. Bonds lose market value when rates rise and gain value when rates fall.

bond fund A mutual fund with a portfolio of fixed-income securities. The fund may invest in U.S. government, corporate, municipal, or junk bonds or other forms of fixed-income securities. The objective of the fund is to earn income rather than growth of principal.

bond premium The difference between the face amount of the bond and current market price. If rates rise, the price of a bond can decrease to allow investors to earn current market rates (discounted bond). If rates fall, the price of the bond can increase (premium bond).

break in service A condition in a company pension plan in which an employee leaves a job and is no longer covered under the plan and then returns to the same company.

bull market A market in which prices are rising or are expected to rise.

callable bond A bond that gives the issuer the right to call the bond and repay the principal before the stated maturity date.

capital gains Profits from rising prices on an asset. Capital gains taxes apply to an asset held for more than one year and are not paid until the asset is sold.

cash management account Offered by brokers to allow you to invest part of your money and hold the balance in interest-bearing accounts.

cash surrender value The amount an insurance company will pay if a policy is canceled before death. Normally called the "guaranteed surrender value."

certified financial planner (CFP) A financial planner who has completed a course of study and received the CFP professional designation.

certified public accountant (CPA) An individual who has met the requirements to be licensed by the state as an accountant.

chartered financial consultant (ChFC) A financial planner who has completed a course of study and received the ChFC professional designation.

chartered life underwriter (CLU) A life insurance agent who has completed a course of study and received the CLU professional designation.

closed-end fund A mutual fund whose shares trade on stock exchanges as common stock, unlike an open-end fund whose shares are bought and sold directly through the mutual fund.

compound interest The amount earned on an investment plus the accumulated interest or dividends. This occurs when you reinvest interest income or capital gains dividends and allow the investment to grow more rapidly.

contrarian A person who believes that no matter what the public thinks the securities market will move in the opposite direction.

convertibles Bonds, debentures, or preferred stock that may be exchanged or converted into common stock. This usually happens when stock prices rise and the convertible ratio is fixed.

cooling-off period A period, usually three days, in which a buyer may cancel a purchase.

correction A decline in security prices, when the market is *correcting* for past gains.

cost-of-living adjustment An increase in benefits in a retirement plan or Social Security to reflect an increase in inflation.

coupon rate The annual rate of interest paid by a bond.

credit card A plastic card issued by a bank or other card issuer as a line of credit to purchase goods and services. Payment each month may be in full or in installments.

credit line The amount of money a financial institution agrees to provide on credit. Used in home-equity loans and business loans.

credit union A nonprofit financial institution formed by employees of a company, a union, or other association. Credit unions operate much like a savings and loan, except they usually pay higher interest on deposits and charge lower interest rates on loans. Only federally chartered credit unions are regulated and have deposits insured by the National Credit Union Administration.

custodian A financial institution that holds assets in trust. When used in an IRA they are usually called *trustees.*

debenture A bond that is secured only by the general credit of the issuing corporation. It is usually not secured by any collateral.

debit card A card that allows the holder to purchase goods and services, the payment for which is immediately and electronically transferred from their checking account at the moment of purchase.

deferred compensation Compensation or salary that will be taxed when received, such as contributions by an employer to a tax-qualified retirement plan on behalf of an employee.

defined-benefit plan A pension plan that promises to pay a specified amount at retirement based on income, age, and years of service. Typically, the employer makes all the contributions and invests the money.

defined-contribution plan A retirement plan that allows employees and employers to make contributions, usually a 401(k) plan or salary-reduction plan. Retirement benefits are whatever the assets in the account will provide.

deflation Also called disinflation. A contraction in available money or credit that results in a decline of the general price level. See also **inflation.**

discount broker A broker who sells financial products for a lower commission than a full-service broker. A discount broker does not offer advice or help a customer buy or sell securities.

discount rate The interest rate the Federal Reserve Board charges member banks.

discretionary account An account with a bank, broker, or financial planner in which the investor gives authority to make investment decisions, including when to buy or sell securities.

dividends A part of a company's net income paid to shareholders, usually paid quarterly based on a fixed amount for each share of stock held. The amount of a dividend can change at any time.

dollar-cost averaging A method of buying securities with a fixed amount of money at regular intervals, regardless of current market price.

double tax-free Municipal bonds that are issued in the state of the investor. The interest is free of federal and state income taxes.

Dow Jones Industrial Average (Dow) Price-weighted average of 30 blue chip stocks that make up the Dow. Used by the media to represent the overall price movement of the stock market each trading day.

early withdraw penalty Used mostly by banks when a term deposit is withdrawn before the maturity date. Also used in annuities, IRAs, and tax-qualified retirement plans, where a 10 percent penalty can apply to withdrawals made by those under the age of 59½.

earned income Income from wages, salaries, and fees rather than from invested capital. Earned income is the only source for contributions to retirement plans.

Employee Retirement Income Security Act (ERISA) This 1974 law covers the operation of most private pensions and other employer benefit plans, including health benefits. The law also established the Pension Benefit Guaranty Corporation (PBGC) to guarantee basic pension benefits to employees (applies to firms with more than twenty-five employees) if the pension is terminated.

Employee Stock Ownership Plan (ESOP) A type of company retirement plan where contributions are invested in the company's stock.

equity fund A type of mutual fund that invests primarily in stocks rather than bonds.

estate planning The arrangement of an individual's assets upon death to provide for heirs and minimize taxes.

exchange option Sometimes called *switching,* this option gives mutual fund shareholders the right to exchange their shares for another fund within the same mutual fund family. While there normally is no additional commission, the exchange is considered a sale and new purchase for tax purposes.

ex-dividend Literally without dividend. The buyer of an ex-dividend stock is not entitled to the recently declared dividend. A stock that has gone ex-dividend is marked by an *x* in the newspaper listings.

family of funds This refers to a mutual fund company that manages several different funds. Typically, the funds have different objectives, such as a growth fund, bond fund, or a money market fund.

Federal Deposit Insurance Corporation (FDIC) An independent federal agency that insures bank deposits up to $100,000 in each named account.

federal funds rate Interest charged by banks with excess funds at a Federal Reserve Bank to banks needing overnight loans to meet reserve requirements.

Federal Home Loan Mortgage Corporation A federal agency known as "Freddie Mac" that purchases first mortgages.

Federal Reserve Board Known as the Fed, it is made up of a board of governors appointed by the president to manage the Federal Reserve System and determine interest rates.

financial planner An individual who offers financial advice and may offer to sell financial products.

financial supermarket A financial institution, like a bank or mutual fund, that offers in one location banking services, mutual funds, real estate mortgages, credit cards, home equity loans, and other financial services.

first mortgage A mortgage that has first right of payment over any other mortgage, such as a home equity loan.

fixed annuity An annuity that invests in bonds and offers a fixed income like a savings account. Also, a type of annuity in which the periodic payments remain the same.

fixed-rate mortgage A home mortgage in which the interest rate is fixed for the life of the loan and the monthly payments remain the same.

401(k) plan A company retirement plan that allows employees to contribute pre-tax dollars that can be invested in savings accounts, bonds, or stocks as determined by the employee.

403(b) plan An employer retirement plan (often called a TSA) that allows employees to contribute pre-tax dollars in selected investments. Available to employees of nonprofit organizations and employees of public school systems. Works much like a 401(k) plan.

front-end load Sales charges for a mutual fund applied at time of purchase. The sales charges are deducted from the original investment and the balance is invested in the fund.

full-service broker A brokerage firm that provides a wide range of services, including advice on what to buy or sell, new issues of stock, insurance, financial planning, and tax shelters.

general obligation bond (GO) A municipal bond in which the interest and principal are repaid from general tax revenues.

global fund A mutual fund that invests in the United States and securities in foreign countries.

Government National Mortgage Association (GNMA) An

agency of the government, known as Ginnie Mae, that buys home mortgages and then resells them to brokers and mutual funds. The interest payments and principal repayment are guaranteed by the agency.

growth fund A mutual fund with the prime objective of long-term growth of capital, without regard to dividend income.

growth and income fund A mutual fund that invests in stocks with growth from the appreciation of the stocks and income from the stock dividends.

guaranteed investment contract (GIC) A contract between an insurance company and a corporate retirement plan to allow employees to invest in a plan offering a fixed rate of return. GICs are not federally insured but are backed by the issuing insurance company.

hidden-load fund A mutual fund that appears to be no-load but may have a back-end load on redemption.

home equity loan A loan against the equity in a home in which funds are usually available as the homeowner needs the money. Interest is tax-deductible up to $100,000.

impound account A trust account established by a mortgage lender in which funds are collected from the borrower monthly to pay property taxes and insurance.

income fund A mutual fund that seeks to provide interest income. Usually a bond fund.

index funds A mutual fund that invests in all the stocks in an index of various kinds. The most common stock index is the Standard and Poor's 500 stock index.

individual retirement account (IRA) A retirement plan in which individuals can establish and make pre-tax and tax-deductible contributions each year.

industrial revenue bond Also called an "industrial development bond," it is a type of municipal revenue bond backed by a private firm but which has been financed by a municipal issue.

inflation rate The rate at which prices are rising. The two key U.S. indicators of the inflation rate are the consumer price index and the producer price index.

initial public offering (IPO) A stock offering to the public to establish a market for the company's stock.

installment contract A type of purchase in which the buyer makes periodic payments of interest and principal.

international fund A mutual fund that invests in securities outside the United States.

IRA rollover A technique that allows individuals to transfer their company retirement plan assets into an IRA when they leave their job. Any amount may be rolled over into an IRA. Also called a *rollover IRA.*

joint and survivor annuity An annuity, usually issued by a retirement plan, that promises to pay a regular sum to the annuitant for life and then a reduced amount for the life of the surviving spouse.

joint policy A life insurance policy that insures two lives and pays the death benefit on the death of the last named insured. Usually called *second-to-die* policies.

junk bonds High-risk bonds that pay interest rates well above market rates. Usually issued by companies rated BB or lower.

Keogh plan A retirement plan for self-employed individuals and their covered employees.

leveraged buyout The purchase of a company by using short-term debt. After the buyout is completed, the acquiring company then issues bonds to pay off the debt used in the takeover.

life estate An arrangement whereby the beneficiary is entitled to the use of and/or income from the assets during his or her lifetime.

life expectancy The age to which an average person can be expected to live. Calculated by an actuary, it is used by insurance companies to set rates and to calculate mandated withdrawals from an IRA and other retirement plans after the age of 70½.

limited partnership An organization that offers investments in which your liability is limited to your investment. A general partner manages the asset, which may be in real estate, farming, oil and gas, and other ventures.

liquid assets Cash or other assets such as money market accounts or bank deposits that can be quickly converted into cash.

load fund A mutual fund sold by a broker, bank, or financial planner that charges a front-end sales commission. Commissions can run from 5 to 8 percent.

low-load fund A mutual fund in which the sales commissions are usually between 3 and 4 percent.

lump-sum distributions Payment of an entire amount at one time. Usually occurs when an individual leaves a job and receives a lump-sum distribution from the company's retirement plan.

management fee A fee paid to a mutual fund's management for the operation of the fund. Sometimes called an advisory fee, it is normally based on the net assets of the fund.

margin The amount a customer deposits with a broker in order to borrow the balance of the purchase from the broker to buy securities. The current maximum margin loan is 50 percent of the purchase.

margin call This can occur if the margin in the account falls below the minimum set by the exchange or brokerage firm. The customer must deposit enough money or securities to bring the margin account up to the minimum amount required. If the margin call is not met, the securities may be sold.

market order An order given to a broker to buy or sell securities at the best available price.

mark to market The value of an account based on the most recent closing price of the securities held. Margin accounts are marked to market to ensure they meet the minimum requirements.

money market fund A mutual fund (banks call it a money market account) that invests in short-term money market instruments. The investor is free to make withdrawals any time and the value of the investment is always equal to the original principal plus any earned interest income.

mortgage-backed securities Securities backed by mortgages. Investors receive payment from the interest and principal on the underlying mortgages.

municipal bond A bond issued by a state, city, or county government or other public agency. Most municipal bond interest income is free of federal and state income taxes.

municipal bond fund A mutual fund that invests in municipal bonds. The funds include money market, short-term, medium-term, and high-income long-term bonds.

municipal bond insurance Two major groups of insurers, the American Municipal Bond Assurance Corporation (AMBAC) and the Municipal Bond Insurance Association (MBIA), insure the timely payment of interest and the payment of principal.

National Association of Securities Dealers (NASD) An association of brokers and dealers in the over-the-counter market.

National Association of Securities Dealers Automated Quotation (NASDAQ) An automated information quote system that gives brokers current price quotations of over-the-counter securities.

National Credit Union Administration (NCUA) A government agency, like the FDIC for banks, that insures credit union deposits up to $100,000 per named account.

net asset value (NAV) The price at which you can buy or sell shares of mutual funds. The NAV per-share price is quoted in the newspapers each day.

New York Stock Exchange (NYSE) Known as the "big board," the NYSE lists many of the major corporations in the United States.

no-load fund An open-end mutual fund that sells shares directly to investors without a sale charge.

noncallable Usually refers to a bond that the issuer can't call or redeem before a stated time or maturity.

odd lot The purchase of less than 100 shares of common stock.

open-end mutual fund A mutual fund that continually creates new shares on demand. Investors buy and sell the fund shares from the mutual fund company at the net asset value. The opposite is a **closed-end mutual fund,** which issues a limited number of shares that are traded on a stock exchange.

option The right to buy (call) or sell (put) a certain amount of stock at a given price (strike price) for a certain period of time.

passbook account A type of bank savings account that works like a money market account.

Pension Benefit Guaranty Corporation (PBGC) A federal corporation established to guarantee pension benefits if a company pension plan is underfunded or terminated.

personal identification number (PIN) A number a consumer selects to enable him to use his or her card at an automatic teller machine.

pink sheets A daily publication from the National Quotation Bureau that lists the bid and ask prices of lightly traded over-the-counter stocks. The name comes from the pink paper used to print the report. Debt securities are listed separately on yellow paper.

points An upfront fee charged by lenders for a mortgage. This is separate from interest or other closing costs. A point equals one percent of the total amount borrowed.

preferred stock A stock that pays a fixed cash dividend, like a bond, and has first call on profits over common stock. The dividend usually does not change with an increase in company profits or the price of the stock. Participating preferred stock is not only entitled to the stated dividend but may also receive additional dividends after the payment of dividends to common shareholders. Cumulative preferred stock usually has a provision that if one or more dividends are omitted, these past dividends must be paid before any dividends can be paid to common shareholders. Most preferred stock issued today is cumulative.

premium An amount by which a bond or preferred stock sells above its par value.

price-earnings ratio (P/E) The P/E is the price of the stock divided by its earnings per share. Also known as *the multiple,* it gives investors an idea of how much they are paying for the expected earnings of the company.

prime rate Interest rate set by banks for their best customers. Many consumer loans and credit card rates are tied to the prime rate.

profit-sharing plan A company retirement plan in which a company makes contributions based on its profits, if any.

prospectus A document used to offer new securities to the public and enable investors to evaluate the security before they invest. The Securities and Exchange Commission (SEC) regulates what information must be included in a prospectus.

qualified retirement plan A retirement plan that is tax-qualified by the IRS and permits tax-deductible contributions and deferral of taxes on income until the money is withdrawn.

Real Estate Investment Trust (REIT) An investment in real estate, such as shopping centers, apartments, and office buildings. REITs are required to pay out as much as 90 percent of their income to shareholders each year.

real return The inflation-adjusted rate of return on an investment.

registered representative A stockbroker who is licensed with an exchange and is an employee of a brokerage firm. Also known as a *customers' man.*

replacement ratio The ratio between an employee's last working salary and the benefits of a retirement plan. If the last salary was $40,000 and the retirement benefit is $10,000, the replacement ratio is 25 percent.

revenue bond A municipal bond issued for a specific project in which the interest and principal are repaid from the revenues of the project.

reverse split A stock split in which a company reduces the number of shares outstanding. In a 1 for 5 reverse split a $10 share of stock is now worth $50. The shareholder has the same market value as before. Reverse splits usually occur when a company believes its share price is too low to attract buyers.

revolving credit A term used for credit cards that allow a customer to keep a credit balance as long as the minimum monthly payment is made on time and the credit balance does not exceed the limit of the account.

round lot The purchase of 100 or more shares of a stock.

secondary market A market in which securities are traded after their initial public offering. Also known as the *after-market.*

sector fund A type of mutual fund that invests only in a specialized industry or group of industries, such as high-tech, real estate, pharmaceuticals, or health care.

Securities and Exchange Commission (SEC) An independent agency of the federal government that administers and enforces federal laws on the sale of securities, mutual funds, and the operations of stock exchanges, stockbrokers, and financial advisers.

Securities Investor Protection Corporation (SIPC) An independent agency established by Congress to protect brokerage customers from loss if a broker goes out of business. Much like the

FDIC for banks, the SIPC guarantees securities up to $500,000 per customer, with a limit of $100,000 in cash or cash equivalents. The SIPC does not protect investors from market risk.

self-directed IRA An IRA in which the investor is free to invest in any approved IRA asset. Usually a set-up fee and an annual management fee are required.

self-employment income Income earned from the profits of a business or profession. Self-employed individuals can open a Keogh plan or SEP-IRA retirement plan.

selling short Sale of a stock that must be borrowed from a broker to make delivery. If the price of the stock later declines, the investor can make a profit by buying back the stock.

simplified employee pension plan (SEP-IRA) A retirement plan like an IRA, but for self-employed business owners. It must include the owner and other covered employees.

single-premium life A type of whole life policy in which the purchaser makes only one premium payment.

sole proprietorship A form of business where one person owns all the assets of the business and is liable for all the debts.

split annuity Two separate annuities in which one provides immediate payouts and the other defers income. Over time, the second deferred annuity can grow to an amount that will replace the first annuity used for monthly income.

state guaranty fund A state fund established to repay policyholders in the event of an insurance company failure.

stock dividend A dividend paid in company stock rather than cash.

stock split An increase in a corporation's number of outstanding shares of stock without any change in the stockholders' equity. If a $100 stock is split two for one, the stock is now worth $50 a share: Most stock splits occur when companies want to make the purchase price of their stock more attractive to investors.

street name Securities held in trust in the name of a brokerage firm for an investor. This makes it more convenient to record dividend payments, send monthly statements, and later sell the securities.

tax bracket The point on the income tax tables at which one's taxable income is set. It is expressed as a percentage to be applied to each additional dollar earned over the base amount for that bracket. The current federal tax brackets are 15 percent, 28 percent, 31 percent, 36 percent, and 39.6 percent.

tax deferral The deferral of income taxes on income or gains from investments until some future time when the money is withdrawn. Then all taxes must be paid.

tax shelter An investment, like an annuity or a limited-partnership, that provides tax deductions or the deferral of taxable income.

ten-year rule A rule under Social Security that a divorced spouse must have been married at least ten years prior to the divorce to collect retirement benefits based on the work record of the ex-spouse.

time deposit A bank savings plan, like a certificate of deposit, in which the term of the investment is established at the time of purchase. Any withdrawal before the end of the term can result in an early-withdrawal penalty.

total return The performance of an investment in which dividends are reinvested and no withdrawals are made from the account. Measures the income earned from an investment and its appreciation in value over a specified amount of time.

trail commissions Sales commissions paid to brokers and financial planners each year the customer keeps any purchased securities. The commissions are figured on the total amount of the account.

Treasuries Treasury securities are issued as bills (three-month, six-month, and one-year), notes (up to ten years), and bonds (up to thirty years) and are sold by the Department of the Treasury. The interest they pay is exempt from state and local income taxes, but not federal income taxes.

triple tax-free fund A municipal bond fund that pays interest that is exempt from federal, state, and local or city income taxes.

unlisted A security, usually a stock, that is not traded on a stock exchange. These stocks normally trade in the pink sheets in the over-the-counter market.

variable annuity A type of insurance company annuity that, unlike a fixed annuity, which invests in bonds for a specified interest income, invests in stocks and other securities whose returns can vary from year to year.

variable life insurance A life insurance policy that lets you direct your investments into stocks and other securities through the use of mutual funds. In contrast, a whole life policy allows the insurer to invest the money and earn a fixed income to build cash values.

vested benefits The amount of money or securities in a company retirement plan that belongs to the employee when he or she leaves the job. The amount of vested benefits will depend on the previous contributions and the vesting schedule in the retirement plan. Vesting refers to company contributions; employee contributions are fully vested and will be returned to the worker.

volatility The rate at which fund share prices tend to move up and down in response to market changes. An aggressive mutual fund's share prices tend to be highly volatile because it invests in high-risk new ventures and undervalued companies whose own share prices can fluctuate widely over time.

warrant A security, usually a bond or preferred stock, that allows the owner the privilege of buying a specified number of shares of stock at a fixed price, usually for a period of years.

whole life insurance A life insurance policy in which premiums are fixed for the life of the insured and cash values build up inside the policy.

wire transfer The ability to send money from an investment to a bank by electronic transfer.

yield The income paid or earned divided by its current price. If a $30 stock is paying a yearly dividend of $1.50, it has a 5 percent yield.

zero coupon bond A bond that pays no current interest and is sold at a discount from face value. At maturity, all compounded interest is paid and the bondholder collects the full face value of the bond.

INDEX

SHARE IT WITH OTHERS

Jim and Richard Jorgensen's book is available at special quantity discounts for bulk purchases for sales promotions, premiums, fund-raising, or educational use.

To inquire about Jim Jorgensen or Richard Jorgensen as a keynote speaker or seminar leader, or for your next sales meeting or convention, or to find out more about Jim's Portfolio Investing and separately managed accounts, please call 1-800-558-4558, or log onto www.financialsavvy.com or e-mail info@financialsavvy.com.

ABOUT THE AUTHORS

JAMES JORGENSEN has over thirty years' experience in financial planning, as a broker and an investment consultant. He is the author of six books on personal finance, including *The Graying of America.* He has been a radio host on WOR in New York and ABC and CBS in San Francisco. For the past seven years he has been co-host of *It's Your Money,* a nationwide radio talk show on stations from Anchorage to Boston and worldwide on the Internet on www.financialsavvy.com from 9 A.M. to 11 A.M. Pacific, noon to 2 P.M. Eastern.

Jim is a frequent speaker at conventions and meetings and brings his down-to-earth study of investing on Wall Street and economic forecasts to audiences worldwide. He provides employees with information on their company retirement plans, and his talk is on video with a workbook for employees in other locations. He writes a weekly "Financial Savvy Report" and extensively covers the investing and economic field. He and his wife reside in the San Francisco Bay area.

RICH JORGENSEN has been an executive in the computer and electronic industry for over twenty years, and he now directs strategy for some of the world's largest computer and technology companies. He is also co-host of the nationwide radio show *It's Your Money,* where he uses his Silicon Valley contacts to cover computers and technology.

Rich has also been active in corporate management and personal finance and is a freelance writer covering the auto and consumer product industry. He and his wife reside in San Jose, California.

If you would like to learn more about portfolio investing, where to listen to Jim and Rich on the radio, how to receive their weekly stock market report, or how to contact them for speaking engagements, log onto www.financialsavvy.com, e-mail info@financialsavvy.com, or call 1-800-558-4558.